ADVANCE REVIEWS

"In *Women's Wisdom: Pass It On!* Kathleen Vestal Logan creates a compilation of life experiences that indeed transforms into a volume of wisdom. As she talks about such things as how to embrace our grief as it visits routinely, how to become our own catalyst for the changes we desire, and how to delete envy by just starting over, she also reminds us that we can go ahead and feed our 'gorilla' to keep life in balance. The best part is she walks right along with us, searching for the place we all desire: the state of joy."

  ~ *Linda Wasserman*, Publisher, Pelican Press Pensacola

"'Moving forward' after the death of my husband has been very difficult. Kathleen's book transcends the many layers of a woman's life in a most positive light. *Women's Wisdom* also lets me realize how to extract the positives from the negatives for a productive and happy life despite my loss."

  ~ *Susan Vanhook*, retired educator and counselor

"Kathleen Logan is a champion for people reaching for their full potential and goals in life, especially women. Her words are insightful, candid and uplifting. She gives realistic methods and shares success stories that empower us all to be better individuals."

  - *Mandy B. Fernandez*, marketing professional, writer

"Kathleen Logan has long demonstrated a deep understanding of the challenges women face as they age. She has been a strong voice for the members of The Transition Network (TTN) who are transitioning from their primary career to whatever is next. Kathleen offers women the comfort of knowing that they are not alone in their quest for a meaningful life even as she challenges them to be bold and take a chance."

- *Susan Collins*, Executive Director, The Transition Network

"After traveling the world for the past twenty years and retiring just three months shy of my 40th birthday, *Women's Wisdom, Pass It On!* is a breath of fresh air, ushering in a whole new era for me. It's sophisticated, yet keeps me grounded, helping me to look and feel alive and happy about life in general. With soulful stories steeped in a grand sense of history, along with an heirloom quality of artistry and distinction, this book is a labor of love. Readers will want to pass it on to any generation of ladies they know."

~ *Jessica L. Vestal*

"Kathleen's guided discussions at Angel's Garden have inspired countless women to believe in themselves, to know that they have worth and a voice and choices. When they leave a gathering, they feel special, beautiful, and more confident. Over time, I've seen several women grow from broken to whole, thanks in part to the consistent positive affirmations they received from Kathleen. Reading *Women's Wisdom: Pass It On!* and sharing it with others you care about is the next best thing to being there in person."

~ *Deb Tracy,* Owner, Angel's Garden Gift Shop, FL

"I found Kathleen's book to be amazingly insightful and just what I needed as a woman trying to navigate my world. I highly recommend it to any woman who wants to be inspired and enlightened."

~ *Leanna Conley,* author of *War Stories: A Father Talks to His Daughter*

"This book is a wonderfully solid platform for any woman to use to spring forward with confidence toward happiness. It shows that at every step of life's journey, it's about personal choices. The book is also just good reading."

~ *Ann Gulling-Simmons,* interior designer

ALSO BY KATHLEEN VESTAL LOGAN

Second Blooming for Women:
Growing a Life that Matters after Fifty
with co-author E.L. (Betsy) Smith, Ph.D.

Women's
W I S D O M
pass it on!

Jennifer —
Keep sharing your
talents and wisdom!

KATHLEEN VESTAL LOGAN

Kathleen V. Logan

Second Blooming Books
A Wyatt-MacKenzie Imprint

Women's Wisdom:
Pass It On!

ISBN: 978-1-942545-04-0

Library of Congress Control Number: 2015938680

Grateful acknowledgement is made to the following publisher for permission to quote copyrighted material:

Simple Abundance: A Daybook of Comfort and Joy by Sarah Ban Breathnach, New York: Hachette Book Group, 1995, 2005, for epigraph.

If there are any concerns regarding the use of a quote or reference, please contact the publisher with your request.

I am also indebted to:
Derek Ferebee for the beautiful photography

www.secondbloomingforwomen.com

Second Blooming Books
A Wyatt-MacKenzie Imprint

Second Blooming Books
A Wyatt-MacKenzie Imprint
www.wyattmackenzie.com

For
Lauren Elizabeth Logan and
Caroline Elizabeth Logan

Beloved granddaughters

May you flourish and grow wise

"Women are artists of the everyday. The world does not acknowledge or applaud everyday art, so we must. We are the keepers of a sacred truth. We must cherish this wisdom and pass it on to those we love."

~ Sarah Ban Breathnach

CONTENTS

PART IV
Building Resilience for Life's Challenges

PART V
Nurturing Rewarding Relationships

PART VI
What's Next? Looking to Your Future

PREFACE

Life can be exhilarating and exhausting, joyful and heart breaking. A perfect, always-happy life does not exist, yet still we strive to become whole. Most women have in common a desire for love and affection, rewarding relationships, to be of value, to raise decent children and grandchildren, to live meaningful lives. We seek purpose, character, and our own identity. We generously share our favorite recipes for cooking, so why not help each other by sharing our wisdom, too?

Sarah Ban Breathnach believes, "Women are artists of the everyday. We are keepers of the sacred truth. We must cherish this wisdom and pass it on to those we love."[1] That idea of living and learning in community is what motivated me to publish this book. When I ask women if they'd like to be in their twenties again, they invariably answer with the caveat, "Only if I could know what I know now!" Well, that's impossible.

Life doesn't come at us as a single math problem with one correct answer, but more like a play, scene by scene, over many years. At this point, my life—like yours— has had many scenes; maybe what I've learned along the way could help other women skip some of the difficult ones, or at least manage them better, as well as show the wonderful opportunities that come with every passing year. Why should we all have to travel alone, figuring life out by ourselves? Isn't a trip more fun with a friend? What if we shared our wisdom, encouraging and nurturing each other at every age and across generations? This book is my contribution towards that vision. When she heard what I was doing, my nephew's wife said, "I thirst for this knowledge!" I know what she means, often wondering why no one told me what I now write and talk about.

How did *Women's Wisdom: Pass It On!* come to be? It all started in 2006 when my friend, Betsy Smith, and I decided to collaborate on writing *Second Blooming for Women: Growing a Life that Matters after Fifty* which was published in 2010. (If you're not fifty, don't stop reading! Women constantly tell us to get rid of the "over fifty" in the title because "it's a good book for all women.") Joining The Transition Network (TTN), a national organization for women over fifty, seemed like a natural choice to help promote the book and its message. When TTN's first online newsletter arrived, it invited published authors to contribute a monthly column, which I have done ever since. Most of those pieces are contained in *Women's Wisdom*.

Also in 2010, I was introduced to Deb Tracy, owner of Angel's Garden Gift Shop in Pensacola, Florida, where I live. Deb invited me to help host a special evening event at her store which would be good marketing for both of us. *Second Blooming* was the initial topic of discussion, but the sessions went so well that we kept having them, nearly thirty so far. Topics quickly broadened to include, for example, Body Image, Happiness, Everyday Courage, Self-confidence, Friendship, and Balance. I eventually started blending my lesson plans with the discussions for the TTN columns.

As you read, picture about twenty women like you sitting in a circle having an honest, heartfelt conversation about an important life issue. You will find many of their comments and observations sprinkled throughout the pages. If the individual chapters sound like they are grounded in real life, it's because they are—my own as well as hundreds of other women's lives, though I did change some names as appropriate. Also, my reason for continuing the sessions quickly changed from marketing to living out my own life purpose, which is: "To motivate and guide women in recognizing, valuing, and maximizing their potential."

Gaining wisdom, of course, requires us to reflect on our experiences. However, it seems one of the biggest obstacles is that our lives constantly seem to be in fast-forward, with little time to pause, to wonder, to think. We respond to the urgent, too often pushing aside what's truly important for "later." Decide now to make what's "important" to you a priority. Live your life on purpose.

What's my goal with this book? To help build a community of women of all ages in which we can take advantage of each other's wisdom. I've taken the risk of sharing mine with you; now I encourage you to acknowledge and share yours, too. After all, collectively, we women possess an abundance of wisdom, so let's *pass it on!*

1. Sarah Ban Breathnach, *Simple Abundance*, (New York, New York: Grand Central Publishing Hachette Book Group, 1995), August 29 entry.

Part 1

Grow Up, Not Old

1

What's Good about Growing Older?

"What's *good*? I'm still here!" replied Mamie, 68, when I asked her that question. Her enthusiasm about life is pervasive and contagious. "Seeing the changes in my lifetime, they amaze me the most. Like technology and the marvels of the computer age. I literally couldn't have dreamed of them. This is real progress." Sherry, 62, said, "I've lived half a century. Wow! I'm part of history now. I saw stuff first hand. I always wanted to get older. There are so many things to see and do and people to meet."

Mamie and Sherry reflect the joy that many older people take in new experiences as the years pass. Exactly why are so many of us cheerful as we age when our culture views it as akin to a disease? There are many benefits, often unexpected. I frequently ask the "what's good?" question in the seminars I conduct. Responses are varied and enlightening, and cover several themes:

Freedom. Many women are delighted to discover, "It's my turn to do what I want with my life." You can understand Rosalie, 75, who raised seven children, saying, "I'm enjoying freedom from responsibilities and taking more time for myself." Tanya, 71, has found an emotional freedom. She says that while her daughters were young, "I worried that I wouldn't live to raise my children, that something catastrophic would happen to me. That worry is gone." We can now plan our own time, choosing activities that appeal to us. There's also time to take trips, to hold reunions of family or friends, to pursue passions and explore interests often put for years on the back burner as we worked and raised our families.

Self-confidence. When I asked Michelle, 59, the "What's good?" question, she answered, "Self-confidence. I'm much more confident about my decisions now than when I was younger." We've all had a variety of experiences and gained knowledge over time, making us feel wiser and more independent in our thinking. We're clear on our personal values and less subject to peer pressure. We're also more confident about meeting people and taking risks. I could never have written a book when I was younger, for example, as I didn't have the nerve to take the risk. Mamie is surprised when people tell her, "There are things you shouldn't do at a certain age." She said, "To me, there are no limitations; I have no restrictions."

Family and friends. Those close to us take on added importance, both in time spent with them and deepening our relationships. Couples often find their marriages enriched with activities they can share. Mary, 61, finds "great pleasure in family, kids and grandkids, and having an impact on them." Ask people what their greatest joy is later in life and they invariably blurt, "Grandchildren! I can spoil them all I want, then give them back to their parents." For Sherry, "Each grandchild brings light into your life. You fall in love again." Mamie, who is single, said, "I'm still acquiring friends. I have a new set of friends, befriending those my age and not my age." Common interests outweigh age as the criteria.

Learning. Travel is a favorite of many for expanding their minds; others take classes or experiment with new hobbies. "Life is beginning again," said Sherry, even as she was using a walker and was wrapped in a contraption to stabilize her hip. She observed, "Life can make you better or bitter." Mamie continues to work full-time at a university. She said, "I'm always cerebrally stimulated by teaching and what I'm learning about the art of teaching. I'm always wanting to take a class. Learning never stops."

Community. With more free time comes the opportunity to invest in the good of the community by volunteering or using skills in new ways. In 2005, for instance, I took a short-term but full-time job at United Way coordinating hurricane recovery efforts, a job which used my writing, speaking, teaching, and counseling skills. Tanya, a retired teacher, now volunteers as a Guardian ad Litem and at an Interfaith Ministries clinic. Many people serve as mentors through such organizations as Big Brothers Big Sisters or the Foster Grandparent Program at Council on Aging. Others serve on Boards of Directors of various nonprofits. Combined, all of these efforts are a huge benefit to the well-being of our communities.

Focus. Yes, we know our years are numbered, but we tend not to dwell on it. "I don't worry about death," Tanya said, "just about taking care of myself and living with purpose." Most of us accept our boundaries and limitations, using them as a way to focus, to take action on the things most important to us. That vague "someday" idea becomes today's "do it now." It's interesting, too, that most of us have learned after all these years how and when to say "no" to activities that don't interest us or have value to us. As Sherry found, "It's better to give more of your time to fewer activities. I was spread too thin when my kids were growing." One woman told me, "I accept my limitations and boundaries now, and they help me focus on what's important."

Contentment. Regarding relationships, Shelby, 75, discovered, "I've lost the need to be liked by everyone. I'm content with myself and choose to be with people who value me." Deb, 56, is "enjoying not being the boss anymore." Nearly everyone relishes the fact that "I don't have to do-all and be-all for everyone anymore." Mamie, however, qualified her contentment: "Sometimes I don't want to get so content that I stop doing things I want to do. But I have learned how to say no. I have a full schedule with 'me' time and time for dancing," and she likes it that way,

Wisdom. "Sometimes life propels you in directions you don't expect," Tanya has discovered in retrospect. When her husband was in an accident years ago, for instance, she realized she was not prepared to provide for their two children had it been necessary, so she pursued her master's degree. Although a crisis never materialized, eventually the degree "allowed me to teach at Pensacola Junior College." Hurricane Andrew hit Homestead, Florida, while they were living there. "It was the worst thing that ever happened to us, yet it turned out to be a blessing in disguise because we moved to Pensacola, which we love."

As for Mamie, "Am I gaining wisdom? Definitely," she affirmed. "It's not necessarily academic wisdom, just about living and life and interpersonal relationships. I'm glad I see things differently than when I was young. Wisdom is part of growth."

We have a gift of years and the benefits they offer us, so let's enjoy the journey. It takes no effort at all for someone to get old; instead, be a woman who chooses to *keep growing* at every age and stage.

2

Who's that Woman in My Mirror?

Oh, it's me! I shouldn't have looked at myself sideways. My tummy sticks out further than it used to, and what's happening to my waist? I had to let out my white belt two notches from last summer. *If I could just lose ten pounds my body would be perfect and I'd be happy*, I think irrationally.

I know I'm not the only woman to struggle with body image. In fact, we spend *billions* of dollars on diet products yearly. (Imagine how much good we could do in our communities if we redirected that money!) As a way of dealing with my own angst, I chose "Body Image" as the topic for my next guided conversation with a local group of women, most of whom were strangers to me and each other.

Twenty-five of them showed up at the host gift shop for a short social time followed by the discussion. After a general introduction, I broke them into four smaller groups, giving each a different advertisement I'd cut out of recent women's magazines. The ads were for post-birth body re-shaping, botox, plastic surgery, and weight loss. In one of them, the poor woman pictured was headless. My guidance to all of the groups was to talk about what their ad said verbally, what it communicated non-verbally, and their gut reactions to it.

The discussions were lively. When I called time, one person from each group showed their ad to everyone and summarized their talk. As for post-birth surgery, "Don't young mothers have enough to deal with?" With Botox, they wondered, "Are these women going to have frozen, expressionless faces years from now? No one knows yet what the long-term impact will be." As for the poor headless woman, they felt it implied that our brains don't count, just our bodies.

One group found an inherent contradiction in the ad for plastic surgery to "Restore your desired figure." They objected to it, saying, "'Restore' means to bring back what used to be; you 'desire' something else. You can't restore something that never existed and most of us never looked like this woman." As for the ad inviting readers to "rewrite the lines on your face," Joetta declared, "When you do that, you're giving up a piece of your real self, because it's your life's journey that's painted on your face." The consensus of all four groups was that, cumulatively, the ads say: *How you look isn't good enough. Do something. Change your body. Then you'll be happier and more confident.* Really?

Look at the ads in any women's magazine. What do they want you to do? How do they make you feel? And how do we achieve or maintain a healthy self-image in the face of this advertising and media barrage? The group discussed, of course, healthy self-maintenance such as makeup and dress, trying to clarify that blurry line between looking our best and obsessing about our looks. Certainly, what each of us chooses to do is our own decision, but when do we cross the line from healthy self-care into an unhealthy obsession?

Some of the ideas for countering a negative body image that we addressed included:

Be realistic. Admit that we are not going to look like we did at age thirty. If necessary, buy a new belt if your waist has expanded, for example.

Be grateful. Appreciate our good fortune and the health we do have. Most of us have friends who have died and others who have had serious illnesses.

Exercise and eat well. Take care of our bodies; we can all benefit by not being overweight and becoming as strong and fit as possible. Besides, a healthy body is a good-looking body.

Know the truth. Lovely models' and actresses' pictures have been photo-shopped. In real life, even they don't look like their photos.

Accept yourself. Each one of us is built differently. How boring it would be if we all looked alike.

Check out www.ourbodiesourselves.org. There are other ways we can build a better body image. We deserve to feel confident and secure with the bodies we have.

As for that woman in my mirror? I plan not to look sideways any more, only straight ahead—both in the mirror and in my life.

3

Do You Lie about Your Age?

Do you lie about your age? was the question posed by a reporter seeking input for an article she was writing for a major newspaper. In her query, she said, "There are three things you can do if the age question comes up—disclose, sidestep, or lie. What do you do? I'm looking for people of all ages to tell me their stories—who have lied about their ages, perhaps they still do lie—and why. The more unusual, extreme, even ridiculous the lie, the better." Seemingly as an afterthought, she added, "Or tell me if you believe that not telling your age is silly or repugnant."

My visceral reaction told me I had to reply. To her

first question, I wrote, "No, I have never lied about my age and never will, so, yes, 'silly and repugnant' are the right words for lying." Truth matters. Sure, it may be tempting to lie about your age because ours is a society which puts a premium on youth. Older women especially are devalued. Once we're past fifty, we often start feeling invisible and marginalized. Culturally, it seems growing older has somehow become offensive, unacceptable, an affliction to be avoided at all costs. Rubbish!

Growing older is a natural, normal stage of development. You can fudge the numbers all you want and perhaps even fool a few people, but your body continues to function on its internal biological clock. By denying your own reality, you miss the special joys and opportunities that each stage of life offers. When you're trying to be someone you are not (i.e., younger), you cannot become who you *are*. Just as plants bloom best in their native climate, so will you, age-wise.

The Women's Movement of the 1960s changed everything. Women who are over sixty or seventy are the first generation to experience its impact on the later decades of life. As a group, those over fifty will live longer than previous generations, are healthier, have more money, are better educated, have built a wide variety of skills, and are accustomed to planning our own lives. But because this is what I often call Women's Lib Part II, we have few role models or guidelines, so we have to create them as we go.

To my thinking, this is a leadership issue. We are the role models for generations of women who will follow us. Younger women want to see a future worth anticipating, so they need us to inspire and motivate them, to be their guides, to set the bar high for a meaningful existence. We can refuse to be judged solely on our age, because if we don't value ourselves, why should anyone else?

The reporter's last question was *Anything else you'd like to add?* My answer: "I'm seventy, happy, healthy, and living my life on purpose. I find great joy in helping other women do likewise through my book, articles, discussions, and seminars. I'm fortunate to be alive, so why would I lie about my age?" Hmmm...I never heard back from her, so I'm guessing she was truly honest about wanting some lies.

How would *you* have answered the reporter?

4

I'm Not Dead Yet!

So quit treating me like I am

"A Woman's Guide to Decades of Good Health." The article's title in a local women's magazine immediately caught my attention. I started reading my way through the decades—20s, 30s, 40s, then turned the page to the 50s. Finally, I was ready for my own decade. Nothing. "Where are the 60s?" I wondered, turning the page yet again. A different topic. I turned back, thinking the story must be "continued on page __." Nope. That was it. The End. I'm a dead woman in magazine-land.

My mind rebelled. *I* know I'm healthy, fit, active, and engaged in the community. I've (somewhat) grown accustomed to being overlooked by national media, but this is a local magazine, full of pictures of and stories about women I know. In my opinion, to ignore a sizeable segment of your home town makes no sense, either on a personal or business level.

This is but one example of how women over fifty are quietly marginalized in the media. Is the same thing happening in your local media? What about on the national level? What do you see? How are we pictured? As vibrant, or over the hill?

My existence—and yours—deserves to be acknowledged and respected. Sadly, we live in a culture that values youth and beauty over experience, wisdom, and the lasting impact of valuable contributions. America, frankly, has a phobia about aging, but collectively we can change that shallow mind-set. The world's needs are too great and our individual gifts are too important to be devalued or dismissed. Young women will grow older, too, if they're lucky, and we can be the role models for them that most of us don't have because of historic changes in women's lives and roles starting in the 1960s and 1970s. We can show them that women's lives can be energetic and fulfilling at every age.

We can do it *if* we insist on being counted, so let's

take action on our own behalf. Because I'm not dead yet, and neither are you.

"Older Woman" or "Elegant Elder"
What's Your Choice?

May is Older Americans Month. Please don't cringe! Too many of us women wilt at the notion of getting older. But it happens, if we're fortunate enough to keep living. Rather than fighting the process, why not embrace it by becoming the wonderfully competent, mature women we were meant to be?

After my "I'm Not Dead Yet" column for The Transition Network, a woman responded to me saying she had decided to assess her life to determine how she could become an "Elegant Elder." What a lovely, appealing expression of our womanhood—something to look forward to rather than dread.

That woman also started me wondering how to intentionally reach that goal. A few things that seem important to me include being:

• *Courageous.* It takes strength and spirit to live a meaningful life, to take risks, to live boldly and fully in a youth-oriented culture. As I don't come naturally by courage, I have to keep telling myself, "I have value. I still have an important role to play in this world and useful contributions to make."

• *Grateful.* I have a dear friend who is now unable to see me when I'm on business in her town because of her worsening disease. I remain grateful for her friendship, but am acutely aware and appreciative of my own good health. Having traveled to many foreign countries and lived in Asia, I'm also grateful to be an American woman—able to vote, have a career, express my thoughts freely, and expand my personal boundaries. I relish loving and being loved by family and friends.

• *A student.* For me, it's essential to be a continual learner, whether through books, classes, observations or experiences. To my mind, if I ever quit learning and sharing what I've discovered, I'll have stopped living and just be taking up space. Learning keeps me healthy, active and engaged. I continually strive to understand different cultures as well as my place in local, national and global communities.

• *Authentic.* The longer I live, the more "complete" I feel. I accept and use the talents, strengths, and skills I possess, envying no woman any more. Once I stopped wishing to be someone else, I could devote that energy to nurturing and growing myself into who I was meant to be.

• *A mentor.* Whether formally with an organization such as Big Brothers Big Sisters or Toastmasters, or just informally, I seek opportunities to be a mentor. In any job, paid or volunteer, it's important to look for ways to encourage younger people. If they ask for advice, I'll offer it (but keep it short!); otherwise, I hope my choices and behavior speak for me.

• *A giver.* In his 1950 book *Childhood and Society*, psychoanalyst Erik Erickson defined the The Eight Stages of Man (Women's Lib hadn't happened yet). After fifty, most of us find ourselves in Stage VII: Generativity vs Stagnation. We've reached a time of life when we look beyond our own egos and self-gratification, investing instead in the future well-being of our children, grandchildren and communities. Donating money is always useful, but most importantly, we need to give of ourselves—our time and talents—while sharing our passions and knowledge. A familiar, much-loved phrase sums it up well: Plant an oak tree you'll never see grow to maturity. If we aren't concerned for the future, we risk "Stagnation" and, later, regret.

• *A leader.* Our generation is in the position of figuring out what to do with our "bonus" years after fifty. Many of us had careers, not just jobs, so these later decades offer both challenges and opportunities that women before us did not have. How we collectively resolve the challenge to live lives that matter will influence the generations who follow us. Younger women want to see us thriving, to inspire and motivate them, to be their leaders and guides into a bright future. We can do it.

So how will you choose to see yourself: as an "Older Woman" or an "Elegant Elder?"

CHAPTER

6

Fall's Bounty in the Seasons of Life

all—what a refreshing, beautiful season! After the "crazy, hazy, lazy days of summer," Labor Day seems to jump start us into the productive months of September through November. December, of course, is when we say, "Nothing gets done in December; people are too busy with the holidays." But in the fall? We feel energized and motivated by the crisp, fresh air, ready to tackle projects, both physical and mental. While the heat and humidity of summer sap my energy, cooler temperatures inspire me; I'll even pull weeds!

My calamondin tree (which grows small, tart, tangerine-like fruit) has hundreds of tiny green balls on it, and some are even starting to blush orange. I can see the harvest coming, so I've bought the crushed pineapple, sugar, and lemons to make my "famous" marmalade. Three years ago, however, after my husband and I decided to remove the tree from a pot and plant it in the ground, it seemed to go into shock (think "change") and only produced enough fruit for one batch; last year, five batches. This year? More batches than I can contemplate. What will I do with the end product? Share it with family and friends who have come to love it, too. It took years for the tree to mature enough to grow so much fruit; fertilizer and water and time eventually produced this bumper crop.

Like me, but on a much larger scale, farmers all over the country are reaping the rewards of what they sowed earlier. Apples, pears, pumpkins and other fruits abound. Many other kinds of produce thrive in the fall, too. Broccoli and cabbage, for example, are more sweet, less bitter and sharp, when harvested in cooler temperatures. Even garlic is plumpest and sweetest in late summer and fall.

Autumn's harvest time comes not just for crops, but for people. We, too, have seasons in life: the spring of childhood and youth; the summer of adulthood; the fall of the decades after fifty; and winter, the age at which we look backward rather than forward, assessing the "crops" we cultivated over a lifetime. As in nature, fall is when we *Second Bloomers* can be our most colorful, creative and productive.

Poet and novelist Samuel Butler (1835-1902) observed, "Youth is like spring, an over praised season more remarkable for biting winds than genial breezes. Autumn is the mellower season, and what we lose in flowers we more than gain in fruits."

Fall—both in nature and in our lives—is a time of transition and growth. Relish it as an opportunity for reflection, reinvigoration, and sharing your abundant gifts.

What do you most treasure about autumn, both in nature and in life?

Part 2

*Becoming the Woman You Were
Meant to Be*

CHAPTER

7

Becoming Me

I recently had a birthday and am feeling reflective, conscious of having become the woman I was always meant to be. My inner and outer selves are congruent, each respectful and accepting of the other.

It wasn't always that way. For too many decades, I was abysmally, debilitatingly shy. (I chuckle now as other women compete with me for the "most shy" title. I had no clue there were so many of us.) Only in my late twenties did it begin to ease somewhat. By my fifties, it had gradually receded, causing distress only intermittently. It can still pop up, but seldom.

Self-esteem was a problem, too. It seemed to me

that every girl was cuter, smarter, more fun than I was. I spent too many years wanting to be too many people other than myself. Little did I realize how unproductive and impossible that was.

Shy and passive, with low self-esteem...my internal life was a struggle. Did I date in high school? No. Attend proms? No. None of those so-called "normal" activities. But I was a good student and did well academically. Because I was well-behaved and studied hard, though, teachers usually overlooked me. You can imagine how thrilled I was in high school when Mr. Yerkes, my geometry teacher, asked, "Do you plan to take more math classes after this?" When I replied no, he said, "I recommend that you do, because you're very good at math and it will help you in college." Of course I followed his good advice simply because he noticed me, but his advice was invaluable to my education.

Then there was the speech class which I put off until my senior year in college. It was required since I was going to be a teacher (it was that or become a nurse, my parents said). When it was time to give a speech, I didn't have butterflies in my stomach, I had elephants pounding on every organ in my body. I spent countless hours preparing the content and practicing, which saved me. Afterwards, I marveled that not only was I still alive, but I passed the course. And now, wonder of wonders, I'm a professional speaker. My mother attended one of my presentations years ago and said, "Never in my wildest dreams could I ever have imagined you doing this." Neither could I.

So what did I have going for me? Loving parents, a few teachers who encouraged me, good friends, an amazing Girl Scout leader, a willingness to work hard and learn, the acceptance of all kinds of people who valued me for some reason, and eventually a wonderful man who saw more potential in me than I did and asked me to marry him. With each passing year, I grew stronger and more self-confident—more "me." A few years ago, a former roommate's husband whom I hadn't seen in a long time said, "You're not the same person anymore." *Yes, I am*, I thought to myself. *Maybe it took me longer than most women, but I don't care. I'm content in my own body, confident in what I'm doing and how I'm living my life.*

My joy now comes from encouraging other people, especially women, in their life journeys. And you can be assured I pay special attention to the quiet people, always drawing them into groups or conversations because I remember vividly the pain of being shy and feeling left out.

So what have I learned on my own journey from wallflower to author and speaker?

• *Live your own life.* Coveting someone else's is doomed to fail, and you would be frittering away your chance to become yourself.

• *Challenge yourself.* You will grow in confidence and self-esteem if you keep pushing back at your self-imposed limitations. Take a risk; if it doesn't work out, nothing is lost, and you'll be stronger for the effort.

• *Be gentle with yourself* and others. Life can be tough sometimes; we need to support and encourage each other at every age and stage.

• *Confront your fear.* If you're afraid of public speaking, for example, join Toastmasters. If you can't stand being in a swimming pool, sit in the children's wading pool. You'll be surprised how much fear shrinks as you push your boundaries.

You are unique. There is no one in the world like you, with your personality and talents and strengths. *Now* is the very best chance you have to grow into who you were meant to be. In fact, the only and best person you *can* be is you.

8

Losing Your Self-confidence? Get It Back!

A few months after my column on "Becoming Me" was published in The Transition Network's online newsletter, I received a response from a woman who said, "Being unemployed has had an enormous effect on me. Now I find myself in a very similar position that you were in while you were a high school student. While you grew stronger and more self-confident, I find myself losing all the confidence I ever possessed. I am in a position I never expected to be in. I don't like it and I don't know how to become myself again. I wonder which is more difficult—to be an insecure teenager or an insecure woman over fifty?"

My slightly edited reply to the woman follows:

"Which is more difficult? They're both hard, but in different ways. In my former role as Coordinator of an Employee Assistance Program, I often talked with groups about the value of a job. It means so much more than a paycheck, as you well know. It provides relationships, status, security, a sense of self. And a paycheck certainly makes you feel like you're helping to support the family unit. Losing your job, then, can have a significant impact on your sense of identity and self-worth.

"Some ideas for you to consider in regaining—or enhancing—your confidence:

• Read *Flourish* by Martin E.P. Seligman, PhD. He wrote *Authentic Happiness* in 2002 which was a tremendous resource for me when I was writing *Second Blooming for Women*. *Flourish* updates and adds to the concepts presented in that first book. He has great self-assessments online—free—which you can take. I especially recommend the VIA Survey of Character Strengths. Go to www.authentichappiness.sas.upenn. edu. You will discover your top five "signature strengths" which, if you focus on using them in life, will increase your satisfaction and happiness. There are several other assessments you can take which are revealing and helpful, too.

• Another good book is Tom Rath's *Strengths Finder 2.0.* A 40-year Gallup study yielded the thirty-four most common talents; then the Clifton Strengths Finder assessment was developed to help people discover and describe their own talents. When you finish the book, you'll have a personalized development guide to help you align your job or goals with your natural talents.

• Exercise as much as you can. Not only does it strengthen your body, it's a natural anti-depressant.

• If you belong to a church, your minister may be able to recommend a good retreat. (They're not all created equal, so be picky.)

• Betsy Smith and I wrote *Second Blooming for Women: Growing a Life that Matters after Fifty* for women in transition, whether by death, divorce, job loss, or just a desire to live fully. We coach you step by step into self-reflection and self-discovery. You'll have a complete picture of yourself and a sense of direction and purpose if you DO the book. (It's not good bedtime reading.) It's available from any bookstore, Amazon, or on Kindle.

• Keep a gratitude journal. This is hard when you're feeling insignificant and lost, but every night before you go to sleep, write down three things for which you were grateful during the day. You may have to look under the bed with a flashlight to find something positive on some days, but be persistent. No matter how small, write down three things. It's been proven this *will* work on your behalf.

• Volunteer at something that matches your interest or passion; you never know what it will lead to. A woman who was laid off from her marketing job for the Girl Scout Council when two councils merged, for example, volunteered to help Betsy and me market our book because she believed in the book's message. She did such a good job that I could see her specific skills. I was able to connect her with a job opening, write her a great letter of recommendation, and she got the position. The down side? We lost her help.

• Make a list of all the things you have accomplished in life, including education, family, jobs, volunteer work, etc. Review the list daily, adding to it as you recall positive efforts and outcomes. You have accomplished a great deal in your lifetime."

I closed with, "I don't know what, if anything, you'll choose to do, but I do wish you well. Given your many successes, I can't help but feel this down time is a 'blip' in your life, a time for reflection and renewal.

You have much to offer. I do care about you and what happens, so please keep in touch."

I haven't heard back from the woman, but I still think of her and expect she's on the path to regaining her confidence. You, too, can actively nourish your self-confidence. You're worth the investment.

CHAPTER

9

Everyday Courage

"Courage" was the theme of the discussions I led at Angel's Garden Gift Shop in Pensacola, Florida, and at Bay Yacht Club in Corpus Christi, Texas, the following week. Despite the geographical distance between the places, the theme resonated in the same ways with both groups of women.

Responding to my question, "What is courage?" the women grounded the concept in everyday reality. Courage isn't just found in extraordinary situations, everyone agreed, it's needed for everyday life. When your teenage son has died in an accident, it takes guts just to get out of bed in the morning. When your husband leaves you, it takes fortitude to not simply stand at the fork in the road, but to choose a path towards an unknown future and start taking one step at a time. When a beloved husband dies, you, too, can die (breathing, but not really living), or choose to create a new life for yourself. As one widow of two years said, "This is not what I wanted, but I realized there was no one who could take care of me, so I'd better do it. I don't want to burden my children who have families to look after. So I lost weight, exercise, and am in better shape than ever. Now I'm happy."

"Does courage have to be big?" I asked. No. Not newspaper-worthy, perhaps, but it's essential for facing life's constant challenges. "Small" courage matters.

"Is there anyone in this room who has lived a crisis-free life?" I queried the groups. Not a single hand was raised. Courage means facing whatever challenges come our way, doing what has to be done to the best of our ability, and choosing to live vs. wither.

We often surprise ourselves with unexpected courage. When her husband of more than twenty years wanted a divorce, one woman was devastated and adrift for months. But after our group discussion, she told me privately, "I will be OK." She sees where she wants to be without knowing exactly what will be required to get there. "I just got a part-time job, but it's a job and that's good." One step at a time; everyday courage.

If courage is so essential, how can we access it? Here are some ideas:

• Acknowledge the many times you have already drawn on your inner strength, how often you survived and even thrived when you thought you couldn't. Each time, you added to your reservoir of courage; you can draw on it now as needed.

• Associate with people who "feed your soul" and uplift you. When you're suddenly single, for instance, your married friends may no longer include you. This happened to my mother when my dad died. Yes, she was surprised and heartbroken, but sought out other women to befriend and built a new, supportive circle.

• Arrange to have "purposeful discussions," like this one on courage. If you look at *Second Blooming for Women*, you'll see that much of the book grew around such focused discussions.

• Always remember that you have the gift of life, but you must unwrap it to find the treasures inside.

Although our conversations started out focusing

on the courage to live our dreams, they quickly morphed into understanding that "It takes courage just to live a normal life." You have lived. You have already demonstrated your courage in hundreds of ways. You do possess the courage to live your dreams, so activate it.

Picture the big, beautiful blooms that a hydrangea puts out. It doesn't quit producing flowers when the acidity of the soil changes; rather, it blooms in a range of colors from pink to blue to purple to white. When the acidity of your life's soil changes, demanding that you be courageous, respond like a hydrangea: bloom in a different hue.

Part 3

The Agony and Ecstasy
of Our Emotions

CHAPTER

10

You Were Made for Love

here he was, at the front entrance, welcoming people to the nonprofit fundraising event. Tall, trim, handsome, a leader in the community, a man I'd known and admired for more than a decade. After chatting with him a bit, I suddenly blurted, "I love you," then fled, utterly mortified. *What possessed you to do that?* I chided myself. *What'll he think of you, that you're a nut case? Or hot on his trail?* Then I thought *I sure hope he knows about the different kinds of love, or I'm in trouble!*

Yes, there are other forms of love besides erotic. Hopefully, each of us will experience all of them, because love is a basic human need. In his famous

Hierarchy of Needs, psychologist Abraham Maslow placed "Belongingness and Love needs" immediately after Biological and Physiological needs (e.g., food, water, shelter) and Safety needs (e.g., security, law).[1] In doing so, Maslow affirmed that love is a fundamental building block for a full life.

Both emotionally and physically, love benefits us. Being loved helps us feel worthy, validated, happy. We have a sense of belonging as love brings a deeper meaning to our existence. In its broadest sense, love brings us joy, understanding, mercy and forgiveness. I'm amazed and grateful, for instance, that my husband knows all of my flaws and shortcomings... and loves me anyway.

Love makes us healthier, too. Dean Ornish, well known author and medical doctor, says that love has a greater impact on our quality of life, incidence of illness and premature death than diet, smoking, exercise, stress, genetics, drugs, or surgery. He claims that love and intimacy are at the root of what makes us happy, well, and even heal better.[2]

As I did the reading and research for writing this article, I started jotting down bits of information which I eventually organized into the chart below. It may not be complete, but it certainly clarifies our deep need for love. Where would you place yourself on this spectrum? Use a pencil to put an "X" on each line; that way, you can do it again at a later date.

The Importance of Love

Too little love	Abundance of love
sadness	happiness
suffering	healing
isolation/loneliness	intimacy/belonging
failure to thrive	well-being
emptiness	meaningful life
premature death	longevity
despair	hope

Given its critical importance, what kinds of love are available to us? The ancient Greeks identified and described four:[3,4]

• *Phileo,* or brotherly. This is when you like or feel affection for someone. It includes friendship. It's a mental kind of love, involving give and take, and loyalty to each other. It's a relationship of equals, and generally takes time to develop. That tall, handsome guy I know? This is the kind of love I feel for him.

• *Storge* (pronounced store-gay) is the kind of love

that occurs naturally between parents and children, and friends. Unlike Phileo, participants are not necessarily equals though it exists between spouses in a good marriage, and also (if you're fortunate) between siblings. Storge love accepts flaws and faults and forgives as necessary. It takes commitment and often sacrifices on your part, but it makes you feel safe and secure.

• *Eros* was the ancient Greek god of love. He represents the physical, passionate, intense, sexual kind of love. You feel desire and longing for someone, whether or not that feeling is reciprocated. Have you ever been "crazy" about a guy who you were sure didn't even know your name? Eros feeds on emotion, not logic, so it can be as dangerous as it is exciting. It allows the one night stand and can be fleeting unless it "moves up" to a higher level. Eros can provide the initial attraction to someone, but must grow and encompass the other kinds of love for a lasting relationship to form.

• *Agape* (pronounced ah-gah-pay) is the purest, highest form of love. It is spiritual, godly, the love of humankind. Mother Theresa personified Agape love. It is unconditional, given without expecting anything in return. Unlike Eros which generates from feelings,

Agape comes from an intentional choice, a decision to "love thy neighbor as thyself." Being a Big Sister with Big Brothers Big Sisters or mentoring a child in school are examples of Agape. As another example, my husband and I worked with a small group of volunteers for several years trying to reduce the rate of poverty in our county. There was no direct benefit to us of this kind of love, and it wasn't fun or easy, but it was our choice to care for and help people in the community.

Ideally, your life will encompass all four forms of love, enriching you and the people around you. Can you imagine a marriage surviving without phileo, storge, and agape in addition to eros?

Or a friendship which doesn't include acceptance, mercy, and forgiveness? Or a community in which no one cares about the welfare of every one of its citizens?

Embrace love in all its forms. Rejoice in both receiving and giving it, because you were made for love.

Was there an instance when you strongly felt love from someone? What impact did it have on you? How do you show love to others? What specifically do you do?

1. Alan Chapman, "Abraham Maslow's Hierarchy of Needs Motivational Model." http://www.businessballs.com/maslow.htm (accessed April 15, 2014)
2. Ben Kim, MD, "How Important Is Love to Your Health?" http://drbenkim.com/print/articles-love.html   (accessed April 12, 2014)
3. "Greek Words for Love – Wikipedia Online Encyclopedia." http://en.wikipedia.org/wiki/Greek_Words_for_Love (accessed April 12, 2014)
4. "The Four Types of Love – Greek Style." http://typesoflove.org/four-types-of-love-greek-style/ (accessed April 14, 2014)

11

Gratitude Is Good

"I'll do the dishes when I get back," I told my husband as I rushed out the door for my next event. I had hosted my book group's Christmas gathering, putting out my best china, glasses, and brassware. What good are pretty dishes if you don't use them? But they all had to be washed by hand and I was already late.

When I returned two hours later, the first thing I saw was a counter full of clean dishes— my husband had washed everything. What a lovely surprise! My heart filled with gratitude for his thoughtfulness and this unexpected gift.

For thousands of years, religious leaders and philosophers have considered gratitude to be a basic virtue. It's an acknowledgement of the many blessings in life, a thankful appreciation for what we have, both tangible and intangible.

It also turns out that feeling gratitude and expressing it are good for you, both physically and mentally. A number of studies have found a connection between being consistently grateful and improved health and well-being. Gratitude boosts your immune system, too, and even helps you sleep better.

Emotionally, you'll feel more positive and optimistic, better able to deal with adversity. As you demonstrate more empathy, you'll be less likely to experience anxiety and depression. You'll manage stress better, too, when you look for what's positive in situations and people rather than focusing on what's wrong. Expressing your gratitude creates a win-win for everyone, which obviously helps build stronger relationships.

True gratitude is freely given with no expectation of "owing" anything; it is *not* indebtedness. When I saw all the clean dishes, I did not think, "Oh, no. How can I pay him back?" I simply accepted the favor in the spirit it was offered—lovingly, with no strings attached.

If gratitude is so beneficial to us, can we boost our expressions of it? Here are a few ideas to consider:

• *Practice gratitude*; make it a habit. Pay attention to the world and people around you, looking for what's good. Do it even in the most difficult situations. My friend, Rochelle, for instance, finally had to put her beloved husband who was suffering from Alzheimers in a nursing home. Broken-hearted, she nonetheless was able to tell a kind nursing assistant, "You have helped lighten my burden today."

• *Keep a gratitude journal* on a sheet of paper or in a notebook next to your bed. Each night, jot down three things for which you were grateful that day. It will put you in a more positive state of mind and ready for a good night's sleep, as well.

• *Look for small things*, such as a smile, good service at a restaurant, a kindness. As a bonus, noticing small things usually generates even more of them.

• *Write down all the benefits you possess*, such as health, family, money, friends, talents. Keep your focus on what you *do* have vs. what you don't. Interestingly, there is no correlation between income level and gratitude; people with lots of money can be just as unhappy and ungrateful as those with less of it.

• *Write thank you notes*. They do matter. As few

months ago, for example, I accepted an invitation to talk about "Happiness" at an assisted living facility. It was an afternoon's commitment, but it went well and I was pleased to do it. As for a thank you? Nothing. Not a call, not a note, not even an email. The lack of appreciation colored my attitude. How likely do you think I am to respond positively to another such request? Write often and promptly.

• *Stop complaining.* It is way too easy to look for what's wrong, to criticize, to see faults and shortcomings. Focus instead on what's good and right in both people and situations.

• *Visit someone to express your gratitude* for how he or she positively impacted your life. Write a letter if you can't go in person, and don't put it off because you feel inadequate. No expression of gratitude is insignificant; saying "thank you" is always appropriate. I love what William Arthur Ward said: "Feeling gratitude and not expressing it is like wrapping a present and not giving it."[1] It requires action, not just nice thoughts you keep to yourself. (My husband got a big hug and kiss along with the verbal thank you.)

Being appreciative of the good things in life matters. As Oprah said in her "What I Know for Sure" column in *Oprah*, gratitude "can transform any situation. It alters your vibration, moving you from negative energy to positive. It's the quickest, easiest, most powerful way to effect change in your life. And the more grateful you become, the more you have to be grateful for."[2]

Yes, gratitude is good—for you, and everyone else in your life.

1. Goodreads, "William Arthur Ward: Quotes," http://www.goodreads.com/quotes/189187-feeling-gratitude (accessed February 25, 2015).
2. Oprah Winfrey, "What I Know for Sure: Gratitude," *Oprah,* December 2013, 198.

CHAPTER

12

Help Your Happiness Bloom

*I*t's a beautiful day, with a pleasant seventy-eight degrees, a gentle breeze, and sunny blue skies. I'm sitting on our porch feeling quite content, so what better time to write about happiness? Recently, I facilitated conversations on the topic with two very different small groups of women, one at Angel's Garden Gift Shop which was open to the public, and the other at a local assisted living facility (ALF).

To start off the conversations, I asked, "What is happiness? Is it just cheerfulness?" No, they answered, it's more than being cheerful. It's a feeling of contentment, satisfaction, fulfillment, being blessed, or an overall pleasure with life. And as one elderly woman observed, "The definition of happiness changes with age because we're wiser. For me, now, there's joy in smaller events."

Then I asked, "Is happiness a goal or a side effect?" One woman thought it was a goal because "that's the purpose of life." Nearly everyone else, however, agreed with Eleanor Roosevelt who claimed, "Happiness is not a goal, it is a by-product. Paradoxically, the one sure way not to be happy is deliberately to map out a way of life in which one would please oneself completely and exclusively."[1] What do you think—goal or side effect? Can you seek it, or does it happen as a by-product of your chosen activities and attitude?

Ongoing research expands our knowledge about happiness. In his book *Authentic Happiness* (2002), Martin E. P. Seligman, PhD, identified three levels of happiness, including:

• Pleasant life (positive emotions, pleasure, sensory experiences)

• Engagement, good life (using one's signature strengths in the main areas of life; being involved, not a passive bystander)

• Meaningful life (using signature strengths in support of something larger than oneself)[2]

In his second book on the subject, *Flourish* (2011), Seligman added two more levels:

• Relationships (the best antidote to the ups and downs of life and the single most reliable "up")

• Achievement (for its own sake, not tied to money or competition; something you simply want to accomplish, like me writing this book)[3]

When I asked, "Who's responsible for your happiness?" I was taken aback when *everyone* responded, "I am." It seems relying on someone else to make you happy is a dead end, robbing you of the ability to direct your own life. Instead, happiness is an "inside job." A vivacious but stroke-affected woman in a wheelchair at the ALF said, "Happiness is a choice. You can choose to be miserable or not." Another added, "For me, it's spirit-based and being balanced."

Then we got to the crux of the issue: "When it comes to creating your own happiness, what works?" One response at the ALF took me by surprise: "Courage." The woman explained that being happy is not a passive experience, but a willingness to live fully, to face your fears, to be brave and daring in life. Do you agree with her or not?

Next, we got down to specifics, covering various ways to increase happiness. I'll share a few here of special note:

1. ***Know your strengths.*** Take the free VIA Survey of Character Strengths at

www.authentichappiness.sas.upenn.edu Concentrate on using your top five "signature strengths" instead of focusing on your weaknesses and you'll have a happier, more productive life.[4]

2. ***Make a gratitude visit.*** Write a letter of gratitude to someone you never properly thanked. Be specific about what the person did for you and how it affected your life. Deliver the letter in person (if you can); read it aloud. The impact on your happiness can last a month.[5]

3. ***Identify three blessings.*** Every night for a week, take a few minutes before you go to sleep to write down three things that went well that day and why they went well. For each event, answer the question: Why did this happen? Positive results can last up to 6 months.[6]

4. ***Do one wholly unexpected kind thing*** today or tomorrow for someone and just do it. Notice what happens to your mind.[7]

5. ***Have a purpose*** and a plan for life, a reason to wake up every morning. (*Second Blooming for Women* could serve as your guide.)

6. ***Become involved*** in something "bigger than your-self." Be of service to others.

7. ***Do what you love***. Indulge your creativity and you'll be more satisfied with your life.

The benefits of happiness are many, including increased well-being and a more meaningful life. "Multiple studies show that happiness contributes to longer life, reducing heart disease, diabetes and more."[8] Doesn't that sound appealing? So try some of the suggestions above and see what happens. Help happiness bloom in your life.

1. Jeffrey Kluger, "The Happiness of Pursuit," *Time Magazine* (July 8-15, 2013), 28.
2. Martin E. P. Seligman, Ph.D., *Authentic Happiness* (New York: Free Press, 2002), 260-263.
3. Martin E. P. Seligman, Ph.D., *Flourish* (New York: Free Press, 2011), 18-20.
4. Seligman, *Authentic Happiness*, 140.
5. Seligman, *Flourish*, 30.
6. Seligman, *Flourish*, 33.
7. Seligman, *Flourish*, 21.
8. "The Art of Living," *Time Magazine* (September 23, 2013), 50.

Someone's Trying to Steal My Joy!

$\mathcal{S}$omeone is trying to steal the joy from my life. No matter what I do, it's misinterpreted, resented. If she would just change her attitude, we could have a healthy relationship.

STOP! Did I really say all that? What's wrong with this scenario? Perhaps it's true, but just this week, I have come to accept my own role in this drama. Yes, for years I've tried to be kind, thoughtful, useful, and generous, but it ain't working. It's time for me to face that fact, to change my own behavior and attitude. Einstein defined insanity as "doing the same thing over and over again and expecting different results."[1]

Yep, I've been insane.

This person isn't responsible for my joy, *I* am. The more I rely on her and others to feed my joy, the less likely I am to experience it. Giving and loving have been mostly one-way in this relationship, but now I see that I was "investing" in it with an expectation of a return on that investment. My "plan" was to do it long enough to succeed. But as author Marianne Williamson said, "Joy is not necessarily what happens when things unfold according to our plans."[2] Darn!

What is joy and why does it matter? It's what we can feel and treasure if we pay attention daily to what's happening. Joy is not a destination, but rather a process of acknowledging and accepting moments of grace in our lives. For example, I experience deep joy when a woman tells me, "Your book changed my life," or, "I joined your teleseminar last night and never felt more optimistic about life after fifty!" Sometimes, a woman who has read my column in the TTN newsletter will write me to share how what I wrote touched her. I revel in that link to someone I may never meet, but with whom I feel genuinely connected. My almost-seven granddaughter sent an envelope last week with a note saying, "Thank you for the things you send me. I made these pictures for you." They're propped on the mantel, of course, where they warm my heart.

Joy comes from a mind-set, a willingness to live according to your own truth and purpose. "To thine own self be true," said Polonius in Shakespeare's *Hamlet,* and joy will follow. George Bernard Shaw framed it more colorfully:

This is the true joy in life, the being used for a purpose recognized by yourself as a mighty one; the being thoroughly worn out before you are thrown on the scrap heap; the being a force of Nature instead of a feverish selfish little clod of ailments and grievances complaining that the world will not devote itself to making you happy.[3]

Ouch, that hurts...the part about "the world will not devote itself to making [me] happy." Seems I must do that for myself—create my happiness, claim my joy. How will I do that? How will I *not* let anyone else "steal" my joy? I've decided that I will:

• Recognize that I create my own joy. I have many sources for it, including my husband, family, friends, readers, people who attend my seminars, writing, volunteering.

• Let go of my expectations of what this relationship "should" be. As my practical husband said once, "I don't have any expectations, so I can't be disappointed."

• Continue to trust myself, to live purposefully.

• Remind myself that life, like nature, has peaks and valleys, that my joys are sweeter because of sorrows and losses.

• Choose to be at peace, loving without strings attached.

• Not expect perfection from myself, because I'll slip sometimes.

Will all this change my marginal relationship for the better? Maybe. Maybe not. Nevertheless, I will consciously choose thoughts and feelings that lift my spirit, allowing myself to embrace the joy radiating from my many affirmative experiences and relationships.

I wish you joy, too.

1. Albert Einstein Quotes," http://www.brainyquote.com/quotes-/a/albert_einstein.htm (accessed March 10, 2015).
2. Marianne Williamson, *A Woman's Worth* (New York: Random House Publishing Group, 1993).
3. George Bernard Shaw, "This Is the True Joy in Life," https://www.entheos.com/quotes/by_teacher/George+Bernard+Shaw (accessed March 11, 2015).

14

My Deadly Sin

"How many?" I asked Mike. He repeated, "I'm working on number thirteen." That's the number of books he has written! He continued. "I sell one hundred to one hundred fifty books for $2.99 every day on Amazon. I only make 70 cents per book, but it adds up. Once you have a following, they look for your next book."

I walked away, astonished. No wonder Mike hasn't been coming to my writers' group—he's too busy writing, publishing, and selling. Then the sin took root as I thought *He started writing after I did. I've only published one book in that same amount of time, and I had a co-author to do that.* I didn't feel wrath, greed, sloth, pride, lust, or gluttony...but I sure had a bad case of the sixth deadly sin: ENVY.

That sin has stayed with me all week, so here I am, trying to get rid of it by writing. I hardly recognize myself because typically I'm an encourager, cheering people on with whatever they are trying to accomplish. I celebrate their successes with genuine joy. But now? Envy. A sense of losing the competition...and I didn't even know there was a competition. Resentment isn't an issue as I'm truly happy Mike has done so well; I just covet his productivity.

There's a real downside to being envious. I instantly felt my self-esteem slip and my sense of accomplishment shrink. If this continues, it may rob me of the happiness and satisfaction I've experienced so far. Then there's the scary picture Dante paints in *Purgatory* where the punishment for envious people is to have their eyes sewn shut with wire. Definitely not good for a writer.

What to do? Continue to let envy poison me, or change something? One choice is to "count my blessings" by looking at what I have accomplished. Yes, progress sometimes seems slow, but it is happening. Betsy and I have sold more than three thousand books so far, and been featured on several radio and television shows as well as teleseminars. The book has garnered national recognition, and just this summer, I won 3rd place for Chapter 2 in the Writers-Editors Network International Writing Competition. Speaking opportunities are increasing, too. But best of all is when women tell me, "Your book changed my life." How much more can an author be rewarded than that?

I've read that "greatness lies in following your own path." Obviously, Mike's and my paths and purposes diverge. He writes killer-thrillers to entertain while I focus on self-help. Comparisons are futile, and I must appreciate the value of my own chosen path.

His success can weigh on me or I can use it as an inspiration to do better, to motivate myself. For starters, I have an e-book nearly ready to be published. It gathers a dozen of my TTN columns in one place. All it needs are a few administrative pages and a cover, then conversion to e-book format, and, voila! a new publication for a broader market. What's the holdup? Prioritizing and procrastinating. I need to be more like Mike by minimizing extraneous activities and focusing on finishing.

My attitude sorely needs an adjustment, also.

When I start my negative self-talk, I'll counter it with, "The average book sells ninety-nine copies; you're way past that," and, "You're making a difference in women's lives." I'll choose to smother envy by practicing its opposite—generosity—which has the wonderful effect of uplifting me, too. In my journal, I'll take the advice I often give others to write down what I'm grateful for today, and what excites me about tomorrow. Gratitude will produce a more positive outlook.

Where's my envy now? Gone! My eyes are *not* wired shut, and all I have to say is, "Go, Mike!"

Note: You're not going to believe this (I sure didn't), but the first time I typed the word "envy" for this article, the print turned RED and I could not make it go away. I had to start all over!

Closure on Grief? Never!

This isn't a good time for us to be apart," I said to my husband, laying a hand gently on his cheek. Only my sister's hospitalization could make me leave him on this sad anniversary. "It happened so long ago, but it still feels like yesterday."

"Yes," Flack agreed, and we held each other, lamenting our loss yet again. A young man across the way smiled at our tenderness; he couldn't see the pain.

June 1976. San Diego. My husband was Executive Officer (XO) of a U.S. Navy F-14 fighter squadron, working long hours. Our son, Kelly, had just turned two and I was eight months pregnant. On Monday of that fateful week, an F-14 jet crashed, killing both men. As the XO's wife, I was immediately involved in notifying the squadron wives and organizing food and support for the families. Grieving parents would start arriving Thursday and I would meet with them, too. The first memorial service was scheduled for Friday afternoon.

One squadron wife was ironing her husband's uniform Wednesday morning in preparation for the service when her own doorbell rang with the dreaded visit from the chaplain and Commanding Officer. Unbelievably, a second plane had crashed killing two more men, including her husband.

Flack was put in charge of the accident investigations so he disappeared for the entire weekend. Depression gripped everyone. It wasn't easy, then, to poke my husband awake early Monday morning, June 28. "My water broke," I practically apologized. Our lives had no room for another crisis.

Since Kelly had been born by C-section, this baby would be, too, so it took a few hours after we got to the hospital for it to be scheduled. The doctor also wanted to give the baby every bit of extra time to develop tiny lungs. Weeks ago, my husband and I had decided this would be our last child. I was already an "old" mother at thirty-four, and two Cesarean sections seemed like enough for one body. It made perfect sense to have my tubes tied while I was already cut open. Now, we talked briefly about "what if" something went wrong, but that was unfathomable. How young and stupid we were; we couldn't see the awaiting abyss.

Finally, the curtain hung in front of me in the operating room, just above my waist. I felt no pain, only the tugging on my baby and then I felt it leave my body. "Let me see..." I said, unable to finish as the anesthetist put me out completely.

Later, Flack came to my room. "It's a boy, Robert Lee," he said, "but he's a very sick little boy." *Oh*, I thought, *they'll put him in an incubator and he'll be fine.* Time passed as I dozed, only vaguely aware of the activity around me. The next morning, the doctor and Flack came and stood on either side of my bed. My husband took my hand. "Robert Lee just expired," he said.

On Wednesday, June 30, we held yet another memorial service for our baby at the hospital. Within nine days, four young lives were cut short, and one – our son's – never even got started.

So here we are, thirty-eight years later, still grieving our loss. It's been such an unsteady, uneven

process. We have had many good years and experiences, but we never know when grief will hit us. It's
like an emotional sinkhole. I don't know when or
where one will open up and I fall in just as hard every
time one appears. My first was when a close friend,
exactly my age, went on to have two more babies while
my tubes were freshly stitched up. I still flinch sometimes when I hear the word "expired." Once when I
heard "Let It Be" by the Beatles, I burst into tears,
much to the astonishment of those nearby, and me.
Every time Kelly has a birthday, I say to myself, "Robert
Lee would be almost___. He would be married now and
have kids," I think, missing our phantom grandchildren.

"Closure" on grief is a myth; there is no such thing.
Our lives have been good and rich and full of love. But
"closure" on our son's death? No. Grief never stays
gone, it just goes underground for a while, ready to
strike again when least expected. With determination,
I climb back out of the hole. Grief never ends, but I
will not, cannot, let it rule my life.

Note: I wrote the first draft of this piece in the
airport and on the plane on the way to Chicago to see

my sister. When it was finished, I sent it to Carole at TTN who immediately responded. She was sitting in an airport on her way to a bereavement conference; one of her sons, too, died a couple years ago. *Shared grief.*

16

Hope

"My name is Peggy, and I came because I need hope."

That honest, intense comment began the night's discussion on "Hope." Twenty women showed up, and I had started by saying, "Let's go around the room to introduce ourselves. Just tell us your first name and one sentence about why you're here." After the rest of the women had responded, I went back to Peggy, asking, "Why do you need hope?"

"My husband of forty-one years passed away in February. I can't see a future now, only a slippery slope down a black hole," she admitted.

Janine, sitting next to Peggy, immediately leaned over, put an arm around her shoulders and said, "I know what you're going through. My husband died, too." Janine had come to previous discussions, but I didn't know she was widowed. Spoken or unspoken, it was clear that each woman had come with a specific need for hope.

I had chosen the topic after hearing a Story Corps piece one morning on National Public Radio (NPR) with a mother talking to her son, together in the recording booth, about being a child and working in the agricultural fields all day, every day. Her family's goal was simply subsistence. "There was no room for hope," she told him. "But one day, a bookmobile came," and she could see for the first time a life beyond the fields. A kind librarian probed her unknown interests, helping her find books that expanded her world. He gave her hope. Even as a child, she intuitively understood Pearl Buck who believed, "We must have hope or starve to death."[1]

What is this ephemeral thing called hope? It's a feeling that you'll get what you want, or that events will turn out well. You look forward to something with a reasonable confidence that it will come to be.

Hope is more than wishful thinking, however, and

requires your active participation. You can't just sit back with your arms folded, "hoping for the best." You must get out of the chair and do something. "I don't believe in people just hoping." declared Aung San Suu Kyi. "We work for what we want. I always say that one has no right to hope without endeavor."[2]

The benefits of having hope are many. It lets you go on in spite of everything. It helps you keep living and growing and planning your future. That's not always easy, but it's essential, because those who lose hope give up, stop dreaming, feel despair and help-lessness. At best, they become "stuck" in life; at worst, they may commit suicide. Peggy was searching for how to stop sliding down a black hole.

Regaining (or finding) hope is not just faith, nor a positive attitude, nor optimism, although those are often essential elements of the process. While faith looks externally, hope is internal, or, as one person said, "Hope is putting faith to work when doubting would be easier." It takes courage to have hope, to step outside of your normal, comfortable space. "I had two choices of what to do tonight," Peggy told us. "I could have gone to my church group or come here where I didn't know anybody." She took the risk.

In preparation for the discussion, I had gathered

some wonderful quotations by women and had given slips of paper, each with one quote, to several women to read aloud. They included the ones used above, plus:[3]

"Hope is the thing with feathers that perches in the soul. And sings the tune without the words, and never stops at all." (Emily Dickinson, poet)

"The very least you can do in your life is figure out what you hope for. And the most you can do is live inside that hope. Not admire it from a distance, but live right in it, under its roof." (Barbara Kingsolver, author of *Animal Dreams*)

"I try to be rational and suppress the hope that this is for real, but hope has a way of closing its eyes to reason and it just keeps growing." (Tammara Webber, author of *Between the Lines*)

"Everyone must dream. We dream to give ourselves hope. To stop dreaming – well, that's like saying you can never change your fate." (Amy Tan, author of *The Hundred Secret Senses*)

"To wish was to hope, and to hope was to expect." (Jane Austen, author of *Sense and Sensibility*)

"In all of the quotations we've heard tonight and our discussion about them," I asked the women, "what are some themes for renewing hope?" In addition to courage, they mentioned endurance, determination, vision, tenacity, and will power. The consensus was, "We are not helpless! We can hope and do."

When we finished, Peggy told us, "This is where I needed to be tonight. I'll be back next time." A glimmer of hope.

1. Simran Khurana, "Hope Quotations," http://quotations.-about.com/ cs/inspirationquotes/a/Hope1.htm (accessed March 11, 2015).
2. "Hope Quotations," http://www.goodreads.com/-quotes/41050-i-don-t-believe-in-peopl (accessed March 11, 2015).
3. "Quotes about Hope," http://www.goodreads.com/-quotes/tag/hope (accessed March 11, 2015).

Part 4

Building Resilience for Life's Challenges

17

Life's a Balancing Act

I'm a lousy example of how to live a balanced life right now. Within four weeks, I've had two day-long book events, including preparing for two presentations for them; a TTN column to write; Council on Aging fund raiser meetings and events; unexpected participation in a major local book event which included two speeches and taping an hour-long television show with the visiting author; an online computer course (I'm woefully behind); two sets of company; and a book I'm trying to finish and send to my publisher. I'm totally out of balance, sitting high in the air on one end of life's teeter-totter with a 250-

pound gorilla on the other end. I need to change something or suffer the consequences.

What can happen when life stays out of whack too long? You'll get an idea by looking at the chart below, which describes "balance" on the left side and "lack of balance" on the right. On each line, put an X where you feel you are right now. (You can do it again in the future, using a different color for comparison.) Today, are you closer to energy or fatigue? To enthusiasm or apathy? Do you lean towards contentment or depletion?

BALANCE   LACK OF BALANCE

energy_____ fatigue

enthusiasm   _____ apathy, boredom

optimism_____ despair, cynicism

fulfilled_____ empty, disappointed

productive _____ accomplishing less
                                 and less

joyful, cheerful _____ irritable, short-
                                 tempered, sad

contented _____ depleted

The more Xs you have towards the right, the more you need to do something on your own behalf before you start paying the price.

What can cause us to lose our balance, to feel overwhelmed with too many demands on us? Technology is a big one, with electronic devices and phones constantly yammering for immediate attention. Too many changes (e.g., job loss, a move, a spouse's or friend's death) in a short period of time, or constant change over a long time, can deplete us. Perhaps like me right now, you may be stretched too thin, with too many commitments and no time left for what *you* want to accomplish or do. During those times, you're likely put off "important" affairs, like nourishing your relationships, while attending to what's "urgent."

But the biggest source of imbalance? Unrealistic expectations of ourselves and what we can do. Our wish to be "Wonderwoman" must go. She's a myth, a cartoon character!

Unless we take action, we're likely to experience lots of Xs on the right side of the chart and attendant burnout. Our relationships suffer and productivity decreases. We may feel cranky or angry, have problems eating or sleeping. On an internal level, we may begin to doubt our own abilities and feel disappointed in ourselves. Clearly, the stress level goes up.

Interestingly, it's not the underachievers who have a problem; it's the dynamic, goal-oriented women like you who want to live lives that matter. That says good things about your character, but also that you need to corral your activities to what you can realistically do.

I'll share some of the specific steps you can take to regain stability and calm in the following piece.

In the meantime, I threw food into the woods for my 250-pound gorilla to keep him at bay, and am happy again on my teeter-totter. After all, life's a balancing act.

A Dozen Ideas for Achieving Better Balance in Life

1. *anish the "Superwoman" image* because she's simply a cartoon character, a myth. You, on the other hand, are a complex person facing real challenges.

2. *Eat well, sleep enough, exercise regularly*, because the first casualty when you're out of balance is usually your own well-being. You'll be tempted to gobble fast food, skimp on your sleep, and skip exercise altogether, and those things are precisely what keep your stress level manageable. Make sure you respect the physical body that is needed to do your work.

3. *Keep track of how you spend your time* in 15 minute increments for one week. Yes, it sounds like a pain, but it will make complete sense as you continue with the upcoming tips. Just keep a little notebook with you and jot down your activities throughout the day. If you miss an hour, don't worry about it, just pick up where you are and keep going.

4. *Look at your notebook* of the week's activities. Write down categories, such as: work, children, spouse, church, community, exercise, taking care of yourself, friends, etc. Add up the approximate time you spent in each category. These numbers will give you a broad picture of how and where you're spending your *life*.

5. *Write down your top values* in life. What's most important to you? Family? Security? Travel? Creativity? Money? Beauty? Achievement? Start with twelve. Narrow it down to your top five from that list, then highlight your top three. Those are your core values and where you should be concentrating your energies.

6. *Compare your week's time summary to your list of top values*. Is there a correlation? If your top value is

family, are you spending enough time with them? If you value your health, do your activities match it? Do you see any disconnects between what you do and what you say you treasure? Make adjustments as necessary.

7. *Set boundaries* and tell others what they are. If Sunday is family day, say so. You do not always have to be available to your employer, either, whether by phone or other device. If you're on vacation, look at it as an opportunity for others to learn by taking care of issues that arise. You need a break from routine to refresh and renew yourself.

8. *Tell yourself, and repeat as necessary, that it's okay to say "no"* to requests that you don't want to accept. It takes self-awareness, assertiveness, honesty (with yourself and others), and, quite frankly, courage. You can do it.

9. *Let some stuff go.* Perfectionism is your enemy. And mine. I could have submitted this book to my publisher a year ago, for instance, had I not succumbed to perfectionism. Yes, you can rework something again and again, but there are diminishing returns each time.

10. *Know and grow your support system.* Identify key family, friends, co-workers, and others who encourage you to grow, to maximize your talents, strengths, and skills. Minimize contact with people who drain you.

11. *Nurture your family, friends, and loved ones.* They are the greatest source of inner satisfaction for most people throughout life.

12. *Make time for yourself.* Invest in yourself, whether with school, music, exercise, meditation...whatever it is that gives you strength to live a fulfilling life.

19

Making a Resolution that Works

"*D*arn it! Where is that stuff I put together on resolutions? I just used it at Toastmasters last Friday, so where on earth is it?" I muttered to myself in frustration. After fumbling through several stacks of papers for ten minutes, I finally uncovered what I needed. By then, I was grumpy, mad at myself for wasting time because I go through this ridiculous routine way too often.

I looked around my office and saw my bookshelf overflowing with piles of books, loose papers and folders. The top of the cedar chest has a foot-high stack of who-knows-what because it has been sitting there for a couple years untouched (except to make it even higher). The coffee table is full. And don't ask me to open the closet where I hide my piles when company is coming and I want the room to look "tidy."

Since it was early January when this happened, I decided to make cleaning up the room my New Year's resolution. Problem is, that's been my resolution for the past four years and it's messier than ever. Einstein said, "Insanity is doing the same thing again and again, but expecting a different result."[1] I must be insane.

So what makes me think this time will be any different? I'm going against the odds which find, as in Richard Wiseman's study, that "88% of those who set New Year resolutions fail, despite the fact that 52% of the study's participants were confident of success at the beginning."[2] I want to be in the 12% who succeed. Obviously, I must change my game plan, do something different, outfox myself. But what? I did some research, learning that people have long made resolutions. And isn't that a wonderful goal—to want to improve yourself and your life, to learn and grow?

My first clue on what to do was inspired by Bishop John H. Vincent's "Resolve For Every Morning of the New Year" on a 1900 calendar:

"I will this day try to live a simple sincere and serene life,

repelling promptly every thought of discontent, anxiety, dis-
couragement, impurity and self-seeking. I promise to cultivate
cheerfulness, magnanimity, charity, and the habit of holy
silence, exercising economy in expenditure, carefulness in con-
versation, diligence in appointed service, fidelity to every trust
and a child-like trust in God."[3]

Whew! was my reaction. What a set-up for failure. Instead of motivating me, this Victorian resolution overwhelmed me and I could sense failure on day one. This resolution is too big; it encompasses too much. But it clarified what I needed to do first which was to "get small," to prioritize what was most important to me. I needed to pick one resolution to focus on. I chose my office for Step 1, writing: "I will clean up the piles of papers in my office and organize everything."

But even that's too vague, too big. Step 2, then, was to make baby steps toward that big goal. I thought about exactly what I could do to change my behavior, to create a new habit which would serve me well now and in the future. Again, I needed to think small. I decided to spend the first five minutes every time I went to my office tackling one pile day after day until they were gone, filing each paper or tossing it in the trash. I even set a timer to keep me on track so I didn't overwork and get discouraged.

If I really wanted to be one of the 12% who succeed, I also needed to take Step 3: figure out a way to hold myself accountable. Since telling other people what you want to accomplish increases your likelihood of succeeding, I told my friend, Tanya, whom I see regularly, asking her to check on my progress. Then I picked a date by which I could reasonably expect to complete the entire project and wrote it on my calendar.

Step 4 is more fun. I'll reassess how I'm doing once in a while and readjust as needed. Already I increased the time to ten minutes, for example, because that works better. As a reward, I'll walk to my local Baskin Robbins for a cone every time a pile disappears. (Tanya cheerfully volunteered to help with that step, too.)

Altogether, the plan that hangs on my desk as a reminder looks like this:

1) Choose your most important resolution.

"I will clean up the piles of papers in my office and organize everything."

2) Take baby steps; choose one behavior which will eventually lead to a new habit.

"When I go to my office, I will spend the first 5 minutes cleaning up paperwork."

3) Hold yourself accountable: tell someone what you're doing; write it down and post it where it's visible.

"I will tell Tanya who will keep asking how I'm doing; I will post the resolution on the front of my desk."

4) Reward yourself for progress; don't wait until the project is complete.

"Each time a pile of papers is gone, I'll get an ice cream cone."

How am I doing so far? I tackled my desk top first and it's clean, as is the coffee table. Already I'm happier about going into my office: no more guilt or frustration, and less wasted time. I found all of the papers with my notes on resolutions and was able to write this column, and the four steps are a plan I can use for other projects, too, like cleaning out my closet.

What would *you* most like to accomplish? Try turning it into "A Resolution that Works" by following the four steps. You don't need to wait for another New Year; start today!

Note: I know I've used the Einstein quote before, but it's just so perfect! It's a great reminder to change our behavior as needed.

1. "Albert Einstein Quotes," http://www.brainyquote.com/-quotes/a/albert_einstein.htm (accessed March 10, 2015).
2. "New Year's Resolution," http://en.wikipedia.org/wiki/-New_Year's_resolution (accessed March 14, 2015).
3. "New Year's Resolution," Wikipedia.

Tips for Subduing Procrastination

his is the post I put on the *Second Blooming for Women* Facebook site in a moment of frustration months ago:

"I need some help, please! Yes, I've posted previously about resolutions and overcoming fears...but I'm a life-long procrastinator which continues to limit my productivity. I'm in Orlando where my husband is attending a business meeting. I lingered over breakfast with USA Today, read my Writer's Digest, wandered around the hotel...all while NOT getting started on the list of things I planned to accomplish here. If you are a procrastinator, too, how do you get yourself going? Please share your tips."

Apparently I'm not the only person struggling with procrastination because my request generated a number of responses from readers. Before sharing them, though, let's give the issue a brief overview.

What is procrastination, anyway?

It's putting things off until the last minute, or not even addressing important items or life issues. There are some unflattering names for us procrastinators: dilly-dalliers, laggards, foot-draggers, among others. We delay, defer, or go so slowly that our progress is hindered or, at worst, non-existent.

Why do we procrastinate?

There are lots of reasons. We may be afraid of failure...or success. One of the biggest causes of procrastination is perfectionism, or wanting the outcome to be picture-perfect, flawless. *If perfection is unattainable, why start?* we ask ourselves. Maybe we worry we won't measure up to the challenge, or the task seems too hard, or we lack self-discipline. Others of us may think we're so good that we can simply "wing it" at the last moment. We've all heard speakers, for example, who tried this.

The consequences are significant.

We don't meet our personal goals, then feel guilty, frustrated or disappointed in ourselves. Self-confidence shrinks. Anxiety or panic may set in as the potential crisis grows, increasing unhealthy stress levels. On a grander scale, with each year that passes, women may find they face the future unprepared financially, physically, or spiritually.

Tips for overcoming procrastination.

Responses from *Second Blooming for Women* Facebook readers included:

• *Know your life rhythms.* "You can't force yourself to behave in ways you will not," author Leanna said. "Pick a time of day when you know you're the most productive."

• *Follow your passion.* "The thing that helped my procrastination," Leanna also said, "was just the undying love and need to tell the story of my father. It was its own entity, more powerful than procrastination."

• *Outsmart yourself.* "I set myself a deadline with some sense of rationale for it. As a master procrastinator, once I hit a limit or deadline, I kick in," said Beth.

• *Renew your energy.* Peter (we have a regular male reader) said, "I take a nap."

• *Inventory your activities.* Beth also found, "Repeated procrastination on the same thing is often a sign that you shouldn't continue with that activity. Review responsibilities, redefine your goals, and pass off duties that you truly don't care about."

Other tips might include:

• *Divide the task into smaller chunks.* Betsy (my co-author *for Second Blooming for Women*) and I, for example, wrote our book one chapter at a time. Have a mental picture of the whole task, but focus on completing it step by step.

• *Tell someone what you want to accomplish* so he or she can help hold you accountable. Betsy and I had so many friends asking, "How's the book coming? When can I buy it?" that we couldn't possibly have quit.

• *Schedule your next step.* Decide, for example, "I'll finish the first draft of chapter 5 by the end of this month." Then write the "due date" on your calendar. In red.

• *Face an unpleasant task squarely.* This is hard, but putting off the task increases your stress and anxiety as it looms out there, waiting for you to take action, so do it first.

• *Quit being passive*, using such excuses as, "There isn't enough time," or, "It isn't getting done." Be honest. Use the active, responsible voice: "I'm procrastinating."

• *Minimize perfectionism.* Recognize when what you've done is "good enough." Not everything demands perfection. Posted on my desk is a sticky note that says "Perfection is failure" because I constantly need that reminder when I write.

• *Get real.* Expecting myself to sit in a room all day while staying in a new, lovely resort with three pools, great workout facilities, perfect weather, and temptations everywhere was clearly unrealistic.

We need to recognize our accomplishments, too. Sometimes I'm so focused on what I have not done that I forget to acknowledge what I *have* done. Gentle reminders from two Facebook readers helped me regain a healthier outlook. "Knowing how much you do accomplish," said Mary, "you should probably be telling yourself it is okay to slow down and relax." And Ladell added, "You enjoyed what you did...lingering, reading, wandering. What a nice way to spend time! Find joy in that."

Don't Be Blindsided by Change

*H*ave you ever been blindsided by change? Like when your son dropped out of college, your unmarried daughter came home pregnant, you were unexpectedly let go from your job, or a friend died suddenly? If you are aware of what to expect from the change process, that's less likely to happen. When a change first happens, women often say they feel off balance or out of control. They typically experience varying levels of anxiety, frustration, and anger. Fear plays a huge role for many women: How will I survive? Can I do this? Do I have my family's support? What if I fail? What if I made the wrong choice? And that can come even when you *choose* to make a change.

Sometimes you have little or no choice. My friend Nancy's husband, for example, was recently transferred unexpectedly to another state. She has moved several times and is an accomplished woman in many venues, but this time she thought they'd be staying in their home until he retired. After years of living in other countries, she finally had her family nearby. "I got really depressed," she confided. "A couple days, I couldn't even get out of bed. That's why you haven't seen me." She continued to feel confused, irritable, and insecure.

Nancy's behavior shows how inconsistent our reactions can be, depending on circumstances. "I've known nothing but change," shared Beth. "I've had to adapt. Sometimes I handle it gracefully, sometimes I don't." And, yes, your feelings may be mixed, with such emotions as anxiety and excitement co-existing, like when you find out you've been promoted.

Be aware that when you experience or initiate a change, your family and friends' lives are affected, too, because for every action, there is a reaction. When I went to work full-time at our local United Way after two deadly hurricane seasons, my husband, who had just retired, picked up the household chores by shopping, cooking and doing the laundry (the ironing skill, however, eluded him). This was a positive, supportive response, but when other men heard what he was doing, some said, "No way. I couldn't do that." In them, my change in work status would have provoked a different reaction: resistance and resentment.

Take time now to consider how you can prepare your family and friends for any life changes you want to make. How is each person likely to react? What can you do to minimize any negative reactions and engage their support? How can you help them see the potential benefits to themselves as well as to you?

As women, we often put our own desires on the back burner as we took care of our families and worked during the "responsible" mid-life years, so it can feel awkward to say, "At this point in my life, I want to _____." It may feel uncomfortable to acknowledge this mature stage, to identify your own needs and desires, and to start planning your *Second Blooming*. Do it anyway. Embrace purposeful change with all its risks because the potential rewards of joy and soul-filling abundance are worth it. *You* are worth it.

Navigating Life's Changes and Transitions

Whether by choice or because it's imposed on us, we all change, because life doesn't allow us to stay the same. Darn! We can't just coast along when we're in a spot we like? No, for life is nothing if not a series of changes. The one underlying everything, of course, is the fact that every day we grow a little older. It's up to us to make "growing better" a large part of "growing older." To do so means initiating changes as well as adapting to those that come our way unbidden.

People often consider the terms "change" and "transition" as interchangeable, but they are not. Change happens quickly and is external; it happens to you. Transition, on the other hand, is internal and is the process you go through in adapting to the change. It takes time, involving a mental and emotional adjustment. Sometimes we experience a change but never make the transition to what William Bridges in *Managing Transitions*[1] calls a "new beginning." You probably know women who have become "stuck" after a major change— such as a divorce, death, or retirement—unable or unwilling to reconcile themselves to their new situation.

As a military officer, my husband frequently received orders necessitating moves to places such as San Diego; Washington, D.C.; Norfolk, Virginia; Japan; and Pensacola, Florida. Each move meant uprooting our family and belongings, and leaving friends behind. I cried each time we left, acutely feeling the change imposed on me. Although I did not choose the moves, "adapt or die" became my unofficial personal mantra as I worked to make the internal transitions to new circumstances and people. There were other times when I decided to make a change myself, such as starting graduate school or taking a writing class. Those transitions were much smoother and quicker, frankly.

The change process is like a story, with a beginning, middle, and end. However, the normal order is reversed, with "the end" coming first. The first step in making a successful transition, then, is to acknowledge the "ending" of what used to be and your attendant losses. There is a grieving for the past, even if you made the change yourself. You may feel anger, denial, stress, or wonder how you could have found yourself in this position. "What happened?" you may ask yourself. Anxiety and anticipation can also co-exist. It's important to honor the past, flaws and all, and maintain your integrity.

Next, you will go through what Bridges calls a "neutral zone" though it is anything but neutral. This may happen relatively quickly and painlessly, or be a time of confusion, anxiety, turmoil, and disorientation. It can be very uncomfortable as your old way of doing things is gone, but you've not yet figured out the new way, either. It's a tenuous feeling, to be sure. The danger here is the potential for making bad decisions, jumping too quickly into a "new beginning" before you're ready, or trying to reclaim the past. A dear friend, for example, said, "I'll do anything he wants if he'll just come back!" after her husband left her for another woman.

You may find yourself swinging back and forth between where you were and where you want to be. Living with the ambiguity is difficult but necessary, so work on tolerating it. This is usually not a very productive stage, but it's important to take care of yourself, practice positive self-talk, and begin to "let go" of the past as you work your way through it. At some point, you will see glimpses of your future and feel stirrings of anticipation.

There's no magic in making the transition to arrive at your "new beginning," but eventually, if you do the hard work in the "neutral" zone, you will arrive there. You'll refocus your life, regain energy, see new possibilities, and begin taking risks. It can be exciting and energizing. Rebalance your life, be open to learning new things, and celebrate the journey you've made. For me, with each military move, I eventually reached a "new beginning," making new friends and having mind-expanding experiences I never could have had otherwise.

Are you currently dealing with a change in your life? Did it happen to you, or did you initiate it? Where are you on the spectrum from "endings" to "neutral" to "new beginnings"? Where do you expect to be on that spectrum three months from now? What do you need to do to help yourself move through neutral to a positive new beginning? Write it down; take action.

1. William Bridges, "Managing Transitions," http://www.moravian.org/wp-content/uploads/2013/06/Bridges (accessed February 25, 2015).

CHAPTER

You're in Charge, So Choose a Positive Attitude

I almost made it across the three-mile bridge to Pensacola when I heard that unwelcome flap-flap and felt the steering skew hard left. A flat tire, to be sure. I managed to creep off the bridge and get to the lane for right turns, knowing I would be late for my appointment. "It's going to be one of those days," I thought, anticipating more bad luck.

Many of us believe that our attitude is determined by our experiences, over which we have little or no control. In truth, it's the opposite: our experiences are filtered by our attitude which we *can* control. One mistake we make is assuming that some people are cheerful because "nothing bad ever happens to them." Life is always challenging, sometimes overwhelming, and we all struggle to deal with our problems. A positive attitude best equips us to deal with them productively. That doesn't mean being a "Pollyanna," but it does put you in a better frame of mind to solve problems rather than feel victimized. It also helps you bounce back quicker. Studies suggest, for example, that cardiac patients with a positive attitude recover from surgery significantly better than those with a negative attitude. The mind-body connection is well established.

Besides the impact on your physical health, there are other costs to a negative attitude. Your energy level decreases; people avoid you so you won't drag them down, too; you're more likely to overlook opportunities and less likely to take appropriate risks. Stress climbs, as does disharmony in your relationships. So don't let one incident infect your day or life. A customer service representative in one of my seminars wasn't convinced: "You mean, if I have a nasty customer first thing in the morning, it's not her fault that she ruined my day?" That's right!

What, then, are some of the benefits of a positive attitude? They include feeling more:

- self-confident;
- optimistic about attaining your goals;
- able to see and take advantage of new opportunities;
- creative and innovative;
- productive;
- energetic;
- willing and able to build positive relationships, because people will be attracted to you.

In other words, you'll be able to "create your own luck."

Remind yourself that although your experiences are often beyond your control, your attitude towards them *is* within your control, and the benefits of a positive one are significant. Nurturing a positive attitude, though, requires a conscious effort on your part, a deliberate decision about how you will perceive and interpret situations. Easy? No, but well worth the effort.

Next time something bad happens to you, assess your attitude. If it's negative (and mine usually starts here), ask yourself: *How can I see this situation in a more positive, productive way?* Your responses determine the quality of your life and—wonderfully—you can enhance yours with good choices. As Henry Ford once said, "Think you can, think you can't...either way you'll be right."

How did I handle the flat tire incident? After an initial, "Oh, no!" and concern about getting off the bridge without damaging the car, I chose to think: *I'm safe. The car is OK. The tire can be fixed. I can reschedule the appointment. AAA will be here shortly.* And an added bonus? Five people stopped their cars to offer help while I waited!

Dedication: The Route to Success

*D*edication. That's what I see while watching the Olympics. Years of effort and practice culminating in a few minutes of success or disappointment. On July 29, 2012, Kim Rhode (at the "advanced" age of thirty-three) won an individual medal in her fifth consecutive Olympics, meaning she won her first medal in Atlanta when she was but 17. She has terrific focus and practices every day, enabling her to hit 99 of 100 skeet targets in 2012. She's now "the most persistent Olympic medal winner in American history."[1]

As observers, we see the athletes perform their seemingly superhuman feats. What we don't see and often don't appreciate are the weeks, months, and years they have honed their skills to get to the Olympic Games. Talent alone will not propel them to victory and success, although it is essential. What differentiates the merely talented athlete from the exceptional one is dedication to a goal, a commitment to persist through frustrations, failures, discouragement, and even injuries.

Dedication includes fortitude, determination, and especially self-discipline—a willingness to put your life on the line for something you deem worthwhile. It lets you declare to the doubters, "I choose to do this, despite all the obstacles and setbacks, because this is where my heart and passion lie." While passion waxes and wanes, dedication draws a straight line toward the goal.

Would I like to have an Olympic medal? Of course! Do I deserve one? Absolutely not, because I didn't do the work. Yet I know many people who want the "prize" without putting in the effort or making the necessary sacrifices to gain it.

My co-author, Betsy, and I know something about determination in a non-sport venue. Even before writing *Second Blooming for Women: Growing a Life that Matters after Fifty*, we were individually committed to making a difference in our Pensacola community—she in her job at Pensacola State College, I in my position as Coordinator of a hospital-based Employee Assistance Program, and both of us in our civic volunteer activities.

After leaving our respective jobs, we wanted to continue having a positive impact. Together, we narrowed down our options, and decided to focus on making a difference in the lives of women over fifty by writing a book. Neither of us liked feeling invisible, marginalized by a youth-oriented society, and we knew other women didn't, either. Once we decided to write a self-help book (thank goodness we didn't know how long it would take), we had to learn about query letters, agents, book proposals, publishers, editors... and each time we took one step successfully, another new obstacle presented itself. We read, researched, wrote, endured rejections from multiple agents, tossed out the entire first chapter and wrote a new one, edited some more, and (barely) survived pulling the footnotes and bibliography together. Dedication kept us plodding to the finish line: publication. Oh, the joy we felt at our official book launch!

Now we're committed to sharing our message through radio and television shows, articles, seminars and classes: "Women over fifty can live lives that matter in their *Second Blooming*." Determination ensures we keep spreading it.

1. Mike Lopresti, "Near perfect: U.S. shooter Rhode makes it five in a row," *USA Today*, July 30, 2012, Sec. D: 2.

Help! I'm Stuck!

"*B*eth," I confessed, "I'm stuck. I must have a hundred titles for this ebook but not one of them is any good." Beth, a dear friend and fellow writer, knew I had expected to publish the ebook last fall; it's now nine months later and I've failed to make it happen. "Let me read what you have and get back to you," she volunteered graciously.

The little book was a collection of a dozen of the columns I have written for The Transition Network over the past couple years. I had asked my publisher (of *Second Blooming for Women*) if she thought the project was worthwhile and she gave me an enthusiastic "yes."

Something was amiss, however, and I was discouraged.

Have you ever been stuck, unable to complete a project but unsure why you can't? It's a crummy feeling, frustrating, and bordering on paralysis. I'd chide myself to "get it done," but continued to procrastinate, scattering my attention elsewhere. I was embarrassed at my lack of productivity. It was clear that I needed to go another direction, so I had swallowed my pride and asked for help.

On reading Beth's prompt evaluation, the problem was suddenly defined. She wrote: "After reading these articles, I think I understand why you're stuck. I feel stuck, too, and it's because columns are meant to stand alone. They do that well, and each one reflects your personal thoughts and those of others, so they seem like friendly supports. Just what they were intended to do. What doesn't work is stacking them together in hopes of establishing a message or a book foundation, because there is no theme, no thread, no continuity." Then she challenged me with, "What is your purpose in writing this book?" And as for a title, "That's hard until you know what you want the book to be."

I had put all of my passion and effort into writing each of the individual columns, but nothing into braiding them together. It was like having many pretty pearls on the table, sorted by size, but not strung together with a knot between each pearl to craft a lovely necklace. I had thought just assembling the columns was enough. Easy, but definitely not enough.

Beth's essential question to me was: Are you clear on what you want? Is it a "how-to, a work book, is it scholarly or simple, vignettes or narrative?" No, I'm not clear. The next important question for me or anyone who is stuck: "How committed are you?" Obviously not very, or I'd be done by now. I read a quote today that hit home: "If it is important to you, you will find a way. If not, you'll find an excuse." How true.

Next decision: Is this project one I really *want* to finish, or is it just sapping my energy? The light went on. I really *do not* want to put more time into it. If I don't feel the passion and excitement, if I can't picture the final product, it's time to STOP, accept reality, and do something else.

I *do* have a project in mind that energizes me. I've been putting it off because I had told myself I couldn't start it until this one was done. (I know, stupid thinking.) My passion is to write a book about women who are living their *Second Blooming* lives, the obstacles they overcame, and how they are thriving. I even have a list of women whose stories I want to include. When Beth called yesterday to suggest I write an anthology, I felt validated. Now I'm ready to start my new book. It'll be coming soon to a book store near you!

Note: Resilience also means you can reassess and change your mind. I wrote "Help! I'm Stuck!" about eighteen months ago, sure that I was finished with the project. However, as time passed, I decided that I wanted to try again. Instead of just a dozen, I printed all of the columns, sorted them on my dining room table by themes which became the six parts, then edited them as necessary. My passion was renewed as I worked, stringing the "pearls" together into this book you are now reading. I hope you find it beneficial, which was my goal, after all. The anthology, however, remains on my to-do list!

Part 5

Nurturing Rewarding Relationships

CHAPTER

26

Friends: Lifetime Treasures

Judy saved my life. I'm certain of it. After shouldering total responsibility for preparing our Virginia Beach house to rent, selling our car, and deciding what to put in our suitcases/express shipment/normal shipment/storage, or just give away (Flack was on orders in Idaho until the day before we flew out of town), I was physically and mentally exhausted. When we finally arrived at the U.S. Navy Base in Yokosuka, Japan, I was immediately hospitalized with a bad case of pneumonia. It was January 1983. Our son, Kelly, was joining a new third grade class mid-year, and my husband had to fly out to join the aircraft carrier at sea. It was a family crisis. Enter Judy. "I'll take Kelly home with me."

With that, Flack was able to leave with some peace of mind that we'd be taken care of. Judy and I had become friends when our husbands were stationed together in Norfolk, Virginia. When Bill was transferred to Japan, I worried I'd never see them again, but there she was, my guardian angel. Several days later when I was discharged, Judy said, "You're too sick to stay in the Navy Lodge. You're coming home with me, too." She had run out of beds by now (she had two children), so I slept on Bill's side of her bed because he was also at sea. Now that's friendship!

Given that experience, asking why we need friends strikes me as absurd. It does seem that humans are hard-wired to connect in meaningful ways, however. Friends can be a source of strength and support when we need them, helping us through crises with food, comfort, company, and practical help.

I always claim I have two families: my biological one and my friends. The former was "assigned" to me, and I feel an "obligation" to maintain a relationship. (Fortunately, I like my family; that isn't always the case.) My friends, however, are chosen, because we find the relationship mutually satisfying and beneficial.

Not only is it "nice" to have friends, but they improve our well-being. In his research, Jeffrey Zaslow (whose interest apparently stems from having three daughters) found, "A host of studies show that having a close group of friends helps women sleep better, improve their immune systems, stave off dementia and actually live longer."[1] 22% longer, according to an Australian study.[2] Friends also help minimize loneliness and depression.

At this stage of life, you probably already know that there are different kinds of friendships. One way of classifying them that has been particularly helpful to me is often attributed to Brian A. "Drew" Chalker. He said we have friends for "a reason, a season, or a lifetime."[3]

A Reason. This was comforting to me because I had lost touch with Jackie, who helped me survive the first months after our infant son died. While my husband dealt with his grief by working harder, I struggled with depression. Until then, I only knew Jackie casually as one of many squadron wives, but she became my lifeline. She didn't just say, "Call me if you need anything." Oh, no. She called, saying, "I'm going to the commissary this afternoon. What do you need me to pick up?" or, "Dawn (her 3-year old) and I are going to the lake to feed the ducks. Why don't you bring Kelly and meet us there?" For years, I regretted losing touch with her after both of us moved, so the "friend for a reason" resonated with me. She came into my life exactly when I needed her most, and then she was gone, forever treasured.

A Season. For me, a "season" has meant neighbors, co-workers, or the spouses during the squadron or ship's typical three-year tour. Especially during deployments, we spouses had intense relationships, supporting each other during six, eight, or ten month cruises. Then, when Flack had orders to another duty station requiring us to move, most of them were over. Sometimes I was lucky enough to reconnect with past friends at the new duty station and we'd resume our friendship.

A Lifetime. From every job or duty station, though, there were one or two women who became forever friends. Judy is one of those, as are several others. We have shared, rejoiced or endured: marriages, births, deaths, divorces, remarriages, being uprooted repeatedly, health problems—everything life could toss at us—taking turns holding each other up as needed. I'm blessed now to have many "forever friends" even though we are scattered around the country. No matter how many months or even years we don't see each other, one phone call or visit and we pick up where we left off. Joy!

Whether friends for a reason, a season, or a lifetime, each woman has made a contribution to my life, expanding it beyond anything I could have imagined decades ago. My own *Second Blooming* wouldn't have been possible without them.

If friendships are so critical to our well-being, how can we nourish them? What exactly helps them grow? That will be my next topic. In the meantime, make a list of your many friends, thinking about the role they have played in your life and whether they are friends for a reason, a season, or a lifetime. And perhaps you'll want to tell some of them, "Thank you for being my friend."

1. Shannon Firth, "Why Women Need Friends and How to Keep Them." http://www.findingdulcinea.com/features/feature-articles/2009/may (accessed September 9, 2011)
2. Shannon Firth.
3. Brian A. (Drew) Chalker, "Reason, Season, Lifetime." http://www.facebook.com/notes/positive-imspirational-quotes/ (accessed September 9, 2011)

27

Friendships: Helping Them Flourish

Like plants and flowers, deep friendships must be cultivated, but an investment of time and caring will pay off bountifully. Friends provide a safety net for us, serving as an invaluable resource in dealing with life's challenges. When we're in a crisis, our beloved friends show up with food, comfort, a sympathetic ear, understanding, and whatever else we need. They also share in our joys and celebrations. Since it takes several years for friendships to develop, however, we shouldn't wait for a crisis to make an effort to reach out.

Of concern is the fact that a 2006 Duke University and University of Phoenix study found that Americans have nearly one-third fewer confidants than in the 1980s. Also, twice as many people reported not having any close friends to confide in.[1] How sad! So, let's consider how we can nourish and grow our friendships.

· *Be trustworthy*. Keep confidences; never betray a trust. If you do, that's a show-stopper. Without this, there will be no friendship.

· *Share*. Friendships build on a sharing of feelings, values, goals, experiences, interests. The relationship should be mutually satisfying. Deeper sharing nurtures deeper caring.

· *Be respectful* of each other and build a relationship based on equality. Be open and real, with no false fronts. Appreciate what each of you brings to the relationship. There's no room for competitiveness or jealousy; instead, seek and applaud the best in each other, valuing your differences and contributions as human beings.

· *Support each other*. This is the heart of friendship—the desire and willingness to share both the joys and sorrows of life. When Betsy and I launched our book, *Second Blooming for Women: Growing a Life that Matters after Fifty*, seventy friends showed up to help celebrate our accomplishment. They still cheer us on!

· *Listen*. Pay attention to what your friend is saying rather than preparing your response. Communication is a two-way proposition, so you should be talking and listening. Unless specifically asked for advice, you usually don't need to worry about solving your friend's problem. More often than not, she just wants you to listen with empathy.

· *Be tolerant.* And patient, accepting, forgiving...you choose the words. We all have our "moments" when we mess up, make a mistake, speak in anger, or aren't very lovable, so let's try to not be hypercritical. Because women are reputed to be better at friendship, we sometimes hold ourselves to a higher standard. One mistake and the friendship is over. Let's take a deep breath and allow room for stumbles.

· *Show up* when you're needed, physically and/or emotionally. Be part of your friend's safety net. The day my husband had cancer surgery, I was scared to death. My fears were tempered when my book group friends, all seven of them, came to the hospital to stay with me. Recently, one of my "lifetime" friends moved yet again to a place where she doesn't know anyone. She sounded depressed, so I'm making an extra effort to be present for her via letters, phone calls, e-mails, and photos. I can't be there physically, but I can be present emotionally. If there's been a death and you don't know what to say (who does?), go anyway because just your presence speaks for you.

• **Be deliberate** about cultivating your friendships. My book group, for instance, was in danger of falling apart several years ago. Once we fixed the meeting time on the first Thursday of the month, we could all plan on it and put it on our calendars. It's sacred time for us, and we've thrived ever since. Another group of friends has a lunch date at various restaurants around town on the fourth Friday of every month, printing the schedule for the year in January.

Reassess your friendships sometimes. Are they worth keeping, or were they only good for a reason or a season? Are they mutually beneficial or one-sided? Are you both still growing? Are your values in synch? You may need to give yourself permission to "let go" if the friendship no longer enhances your life, appreciating it for what it did bring during a certain period of time.

Friends. What precious people they are, enriching our lives immeasurably. More than nice, they are necessary to our well-being, so it's unquestionably worth helping our relationships flourish.

1. Shannon Firth, "Why Women Need Friends and How to Keep Them." http://www.findingdulcinea.com/features/feature-articles/2009/may (accessed September 9, 2011)

40th Anniversary? How Did You Do That?

"ou're celebrating your 40th anniversary?" the waitress marveled. "How did you do that?" She hovered at the table, genuinely curious.

"Marry a great guy," I shot back with a smile, but her question started me wondering, too: How *did* we do it? My husband, Flack, was active duty navy for the first twenty years we were married. He was at sea for eleven months the first year, thirty of the first thirty-six months, and at sea all told for twelve years of the twenty. For the first year, I'd look at our wedding album daily, thinking, "I must be married because here are the pictures that prove it."

We've also coped with being caregivers for my mother; the health crises and deaths of our parents, his sister and one of my brothers; having a niece twice live with us; Flack's cancer surgery and subsequent radiation; my surgery for melanoma; frequent moves. Normal life stuff. The biggest challenge to us came in 1976 when we experienced an anguishing week in which F-14 fighter jet crashes on Monday and Wednesday killed four squadron mates. We met with devastated spouses and parents, and attended memorial services Thursday and Friday. On the following Monday, our second son, Robert Lee Logan, was born a month early by C-section in the afternoon. He died Tuesday. On Wednesday, we had a memorial service for our own child. We were overwhelmed.

Many marriages crumble in the wake of losing a child, so why didn't ours? What did it take for us to survive this catastrophe and everything else? Flack and I had a wonderful conversation as I prepared to write this column, asking ourselves that very question. We decided that, for us, four factors contributed to the longevity and overall happiness of our marriage.

1. *Commitment*. In my sister's backyard on July 24, 1971, Flack and I promised we would "love, honor, and cherish each other till death us do part." That pledge

to be faithful was tested constantly when we were an ocean apart for months and months. I also believe commitment is what carried us through the devastating loss of our son as we didn't really share our grief, living parallel lives for a couple years. Divorce was never an option, though, as we honored our promise until our souls could fully reconnect.

2. ***Shared values***. For Flack, this is a key factor. "Both partners must know that values are important. When issues come up, you can refer back to them." As for us, we value being an intact, responsible, loving family. Money serves only as a means to live comfortably and to do good in the community. Education (we met at the U.S. Naval Postgraduate School) and self-learning are important and our shelves are bulging with books. Respect for every individual without regard to class or economic status is essential, as are honesty and integrity. Of course, we diverge on other individual values, but as a couple, these define us and help keep us together.

3. ***Shared activities***. "It's essential to enjoy doing some things together," says Flack, "if they add to the relationship." He recalls going camping in a tiny rented trailer six weeks after Robert Lee died, just he and I and Kelly, who was two. "That was helpful," he

says, as it reaffirmed us as a family. Now, we love being grandparents, the theatre, boating, helping out at the local soup kitchen, working with others to reduce the county's poverty rate, cooking and entertaining. But we also go our separate ways as desired.

4. ***Mutual enrichment.*** "That person you marry must 'complete' you," Flack believes. "Yes, you could go on alone, but a good spouse makes you 'more' than you are." For him, there must be positive growth in the relationship. If not, "I wouldn't want to do this anymore." I've often thought Flack saw more potential in me than I saw in myself. His patience and nurturing and support have allowed me to grow. Years ago, he told me (much to my surprise), "You've made me a better person." Now I'm in my *Second Blooming* as an author and speaker and he's cheering me on.

Commitment, shared values and activities, mutual enrichment—these are the factors Flack and I have found important in our long, sometimes challenging, but ultimately very satisfying marriage.

If you've been in a long-term relationship, what makes it work? What might enrich it even more?

If it failed, what was missing? What would you seek in a future relationship?

CHAPTER

Kindness: Charity in Your Heart

"If you haven't any charity in your heart, you have the worst kind of heart trouble." ~ *Bob Hope*

"$\mathcal{I}$ enjoyed sitting with you this evening," I said to Brenda. It was a simple statement, genuine and polite, but her response took me by surprise. "Thank *you*," she replied, "for being so kind. I was nervous about coming because I knew I wouldn't know anyone, and you made me feel comfortable."

During our dinner conversation, I learned Brenda was not married to the man sitting to her right, but was recently widowed. We also discovered we had a lot in common: husbands who had navy careers, and children who were now in the military (my son) or married to military men (her daughters). For me, it was a normal conversation, but it was clear she viewed it otherwise.

Being kind matters. Whether in business or socially, it goes a long way toward creating a nurturing, positive environment. It builds a sense of kinship and connectedness, a feeling that "we're on this life journey together." Kindness shows in our eyes, in our smiles and gestures, joining us as human beings.

Even though the intent of kindness is to give something away out of compassion or empathy, both the giver and receiver benefit from the interaction, physically as well as psychologically. Studies are finding that "Being a good friend, and being compassionate toward others, may be one of the best ways to improve your own health."[1]

Individual acts of kindness abound in everyday life. When my friend Mary's ninety-year old mother came to live with her and her husband, their lives were significantly constrained. Bill, a physician, was scheduled to attend a medical conference and wanted Mary to go with him. When Mary shared her dilemma at our book group, Beth piped up, "I'll come stay with your mother. Go ahead and make your plans." Gratitude bloomed on Mary's face.

Organizational kindness exists, too. Another friend, Jean, has been undergoing cancer treatment over the past nine months at MD Anderson in Houston, Texas, a long day's drive from her home. As a mission project, a church there subsidizes several apartments for out-of-towners who need to stay for extended periods of time during their medical treatment. Jean benefits greatly from the church's help and the women's compassion. She says an unexpected bonus has been, "The women in that church have become my friends."

Perhaps you volunteer in your community, also an act of benevolence. My husband and I, for instance, help cook, serve breakfast, and clean up at our local Loaves and Fishes soup kitchen every two weeks. I look people in the eyes as I place coffee or food in front of them, saying a cheery "good morning" at each table. They seem to appreciate that simple act of courtesy as much as the good food.

Sometimes I get discouraged with the negativity and conflict around me, the unwillingness to work together or value each other as human beings. I find I must be intentional about my approach to people. I *choose* to think well of them, to be patient, to lend a

helping hand when I can, to be respectful and empa-
thetic, for I never know what kind of emotional pain
they may be experiencing, or when I will need to be
on the receiving end.

Kindness is a gracious gift of the spirit, free....but
invaluable. So reach out to someone, anyone: smile,
pay a visit, shake hands warmly, give words of comfort
or encouragement, be friendly and accepting. As with
Brenda at my dinner table, a small kindness can be a
double blessing. We both left feeling uplifted, and so
will you.

> Kind hearts are the gardens,
> Kind thoughts are the roots,
> Kind words are the blossoms,
> Kind deeds are the fruits.
> *19th century rhyme used in primary schools*

1. Maia Szalavitz, "The Biology of Kindness: How It Makes Us
   Happier and Healthier," http://healthland.time.com/2013
   /05/09/why-kindness-can-make-us (accessed March 13, 2015).

Trust: the Tie that Binds

"I hear you have melanoma," an acquaintance said to me in a low voice at a party.

"How on earth would you know that?" I asked, stunned.

"The source doesn't matter," he replied. Yes, it did! I hadn't come to grips with the disastrous possibilities myself as I awaited surgery, and I sure didn't want my anxiety to be fodder for casual conversation. Someone in my primary care physician's office had broken a professional confidence and I was not happy.

Whether professional or personal, trust means being able to count on someone to keep secrets, to not hurt or harm you, to keep his or her word, to not tell lies. It's the essential building block for any relationship. Trusting people can be dangerous, however, and once betrayed, some of us put up emotional walls which can *seem* to protect us, but also hold us back from developing deep, fulfilling relationships. To stop trusting is to stop living and loving. Having positive, trusting relationships increases our well-being and happiness.

The first and most important person to trust, of course, is *you*, because that lays the foundation for all other relationships. If you don't trust and believe in yourself, why would you extend trust to anyone else?

Just what does it take to trust other people? Personally, I always assume the best and look for the good in individuals...until they prove me wrong. If they do, I don't let one bad experience ruin the potential with other people in the future. To be trustworthy, it's critical to tell the truth, safeguard secrets, keep your word, be dependable, to follow through on promises you have made. When you do mess up (we all do), apologize. It takes courage to say, "I'm sorry," Be equally willing to forgive, too.

There are levels of betrayal, of course, with canceling lunch at the last minute, for example, at one end of the spectrum and infidelity at the other end. I've had several friends deal with infidelity, an enormous, soul-searing hurt. While some could not forgive and get beyond the pain, others managed to salvage their marriages. "As long as it didn't affect our life at home," Kathy confided in me several years ago, "I managed to live with it." For women who did stay married, though, rebuilding trust took years, and was, as one woman told me, "a conscious choice on my part every day, no longer a given. He had to earn it again and again."

If you are the person who has been betrayed, what can you do?

· Acknowledge what happened. Denial doesn't work; you must process what occurred.

· Confide in someone you still trust.

· Speak to the person who betrayed you; state your position, and why you're upset. (I told my doctor who met with her staff.)

· Work to heal yourself; you may need to put time and/or space between you and the betrayer. (This is especially hard with infidelity.)

· Decide if the relationship is worth keeping and the effort it will take to rebuild your trust.

· Work on rebuilding the relationship or end it,

even if the person is very sorry. Sometimes you can accept the apology but choose not to continue the relationship.

· Be aware that, even if you forgive and invest in making the relationship re-grow, trusting will be forever different because it's now a continuing decision vs. a "gift."

If you were the betrayer, what steps can you take?

· Say you're sorry, but you must follow that up with consistent, appropriate behavior.

· You may need to give up some privacy, not just saying, for instance, "I'll be home late."

· Quit lying; tell the truth even if it's hard.

· Stop keeping secrets which can undermine your relationship and kill trust.

· Create an environment in which the person you betrayed feels safe.

· Ask the person you betrayed what he or she needs from you, such as, "What can I do to help make this situation better? How can I make you feel more secure?"

Trust is the tie that binds us together. Nurture it by being a person of good character yourself; expect the same of others.

(Note: I had the surgery and the melanoma was "in situ" so the surgeon was able to excise all of it.)

Part 6

What's Next? Looking to Your Future

Three Keys to a Healthy and Fulfilling Life

*W*ould you like to know the three keys to a healthy and fulfilling life? They are physical, financial, and spiritual health. Not so complicated, is it?

First, enhance your physical health, which involves exercise and nutrition. This seems obvious, of course, but it isn't so easy to do in a country which grows statistically more obese every year, with attendant illnesses such as high blood pressure and diabetes.

• *Exercise*. A favorite book of mine on the subject is *Younger Next Year for Women* by Chris Crowley and Henry S. Lodge, M.D. Their prescription? Forty-five minutes a day, six days per week. Make small changes in your routine, too, like taking the stairway instead of the elevator. Quit looking for the closest parking spot and take the first or farthest one you see. If you have a short grocery list of stuff that won't melt, walk to the store, and when you get there, go the opposite direction of the items you need. Also, appreciate the extra steps you take while wandering the aisles searching, say, for that elusive can of hearts of palm. Be creative in adding exercise to your day. Thirty minutes a day, three days a week is the minimum.

· *Nutrition*. I never connected with the government's food "Pyramid" so it had no impact on my eating habits, but the United States Department of Agriculture's new "My Plate" with four segments for fruits, grains, vegetables, and protein (plus some dairy) makes sense both visually and mentally. It's now very easy to picture what and how much to eat. I enjoy each season's bounty, too, by seeking out local growers and their fresh produce. My city has a special street market on Saturdays which has been hugely successful for vendors and buyers alike, as well as a farmer's market which is open daily. Where can you find your local growers?

Second, ensure your financial health. There is

currently a bounty of articles focused on women, especially those over fifty, who worry: How much money do I need? Will I outlive my money? How can I grow the money I have now? It's hard to think about a living a life that matters if you're living from paycheck to paycheck or sinking in debt. Both saving and investing are essential.

On average, women live seven years longer than men. Also on average, women have fewer earning years and receive between 77 – 81 cents for every dollar men make. The result? Women have less money to stretch over more years. You have two choices: spend less or generate more. Or both, of course. Begin by clarifying "want" vs. "need" when you shop; postpone your decision for a day to see if the purchase still has value to you. Put any money you decide not to spend in your kitty. Save regularly, making it a priority. Then invest it. Start now. If you need help, find a good financial advisor who is interested in your well-being. I've worked with such a woman for decades and trust her guidance. A practical book on this topic is *The Difference* by Jean Chatzky.

Third, enrich your spiritual health. This encompasses your mental, emotional and psychological well-being. I believe each of us is on this earth for a reason, though discerning it isn't always easy or obvious. Are there specific actions you can take to live a purposeful, spiritual life? Definitely. They include:

- accepting your age;
- choosing a positive attitude about the future;
- initiating the changes you want to make based on your values;
- identifying and employing your talents, strengths, and skills;
- resurrecting your passions and dreams;
- developing your own one-sentence life purpose statement;
- deciding how best to pull all of this together into a plan; and
- taking action.

A book I like on this topic (I'm just a little prejudiced here) is the one my co-author Betsy Smith and I wrote: *Second Blooming for Women: Growing a Life that Matters after Fifty*. Women have consistently suggested we delete the "over fifty" part of the title because "It's a good book for *all* women" so don't let the title deter you if you're younger. It takes you step by step through the process of self-discovery, allowing you to enrich your spiritual health and live purposefully.

The action step for Betsy and me, of course, was: Write the book.

You are in charge of your life; no one can live it for you. If you pay attention to the three keys—physical, financial, and spiritual health—you can live a purposeful and fulfilling life.

CHAPTER

Older and Wiser? Maybe.

"When I am old, I will be wise." Maybe you will, maybe you won't, because longevity alone does not guarantee wisdom. Gaining wisdom—like life itself—is a process, not a product, and needs to be nurtured throughout a lifetime. Haven't you known women who glided through the decades, learning little along the way?

I met once with a small group of women at Angel's Garden when "wisdom" was our discussion topic. "What is wisdom?" I asked. Their replies included:

"It's more than facts or information or academic knowledge, though that's where it starts."

"It comes from opportunities to grow."

"We grow most in wisdom through adversity, like when my husband decided he wanted a divorce. I know I'm the best thing that ever happened to him, but he didn't agree."

"It's a lifelong journey."

Then the group got practical. "As a woman over fifty," I asked, "what wisdom have you gained?" We all laughed when one said, "That my parents were right!" Others added:

"It's essential to believe in yourself. I do now, but it took me until I turned fifty."

"I'm stronger than I thought I was." (from the woman whose husband left her)

"I trust myself more. I'm less susceptible to other people's opinions and advice. I make up my own mind now."

"I know life has its ups and downs, that nothing lasts forever—neither the good nor the bad. Everything seems to move in cycles."

Next, we talked about what wisdom we'd share with our younger selves:

"You mean from me to a younger me? I'd tell myself to follow your dreams and your heart, even if it's not practical. You don't get these years back.'"

"You have value. Don't ever 'settle.'"

"You have potential and will keep growing into it. Don't give up on yourself."

"Bad things happen, so don't be surprised. Just keep going and it'll get better again."

"You don't have to do all things and be all things for everybody."

"Life after fifty is women's best kept secret. Don't be afraid of getting older."

If we pay attention to our experiences like these women have, we can learn from them and become wiser. As Sherwin B. Nuland wrote in his wonderful book *The Art of Aging: a Doctor's Prescription for Well-Being,*

"Knowledge is not wisdom. Wisdom involves the management of knowledge, which in turn involves comprehension of the significance of the knowledge possessed. Wisdom is knowledge put to use by judgment." [1]

We'll continue this discussion in the next chapter. In the meantime, ask yourself (even better, write down your responses):

What does "wisdom" mean to me?

As a woman, what wisdom have I gained so far?

What wisdom would I share with my younger self?

---

1. Sherwin B. Nuland, *The Art of Aging: a Doctor's Prescription for Well-Being* (New York: Random House, 2007), 254.

Older and Wiser? Yes!

$\mathcal{W}$ isdom is a lifelong process, requiring us to pay attention to what's happening and to learn from our experiences. In his book *The Art of Aging: a Doctor's Prescription for Well-being,* Dr. Sherwin Nuland wrote that the ultimate purpose of wisdom is to take action.[1]

To illustrate what he meant, draw a large circle on a piece of paper, writing YOUR LIFE in the center of it. At the 12 o'clock position, write *Action*; at 3, *Experience*; at 6, *Reflection*; and at 9, *Wisdom*.

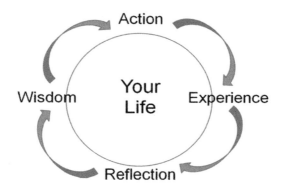

Clockwise, each step leads to the next. Here's an example of how the process works, using a real-life story shared at the group discussion:

Action: Carol visited her two out-of-state grandchildren whom she had not seen in a couple years.

Experience: Carol spent extra time with her granddaughter because her daughter had said the sixteen-year-old was depressed.

Reflection: In thinking over the experience once she returned home, Carol decided the granddaughter was not depressed, but aimless and discouraged because she felt "different" from what she thought her parents wanted her to be.

Wisdom: Carol told us she had decided, "My grandchildren need me in their lives. I can support them in ways their parents can't. My grandchildren, especially my granddaughter, need all of us involved in their lives for different reasons."

Action: (note how it comes full circle) Carol plans to go visit again in three months and call every couple of weeks in the meantime.

What if Carol had quit at "wisdom" and had never taken the final "action" step? Her knowledge and insight would be wasted, and the granddaughter's life would lack that extra loving source of nourishment. As Carol said, "If we don't share our wisdom, its sweetness turns bitter."

Reflect on one of your experiences. What happened? Why? How might it have gone differently? What did you learn from it? In other words, what wisdom did you gain? And what does it tell you about what action to take in the future? Be intentional in examining your experiences because the people in your life need you to actively share your wisdom.

1. Sherwin B. Nuland, *The Art of Aging: A Doctor's Prescription for Well-Being* (New York: Random House, 2007), 260.

$\mathcal{34}$

What's on Your Spiritual Bucket List?

 $\mathcal{O}$ ne of the most wonderful but undervalued aspects of growing older is the power of our minds to focus more clearly on what's important to us and what we want yet to accomplish. We recognize that we won't be able to do everything we had once hoped to, so we start assessing what's most significant. We begin to concentrate our energy and abilities toward reaching the goals we hold most dear, dipping into our spiritual "bucket list," so to speak. But how does that process work?

Ready or not, we must adapt to the fact that our lives have limits because no one—not queens, presidents, chief executive officers, athletes—lives forever. Many have tried over the centuries, using elixirs, potions, or cryogenics, while others had favorite people, possessions, jewels or food put into their tombs or pyramids, convinced another kind of "life" awaited them. Perhaps they were right, but all we know for certain is that life on earth is finite.

A clear focus doesn't just happen, however, usually requiring mindful thought and consideration. Below is one approach I find particularly useful when my mind seems muddled. To try it, have a pencil, piece of paper, and highlighter handy.

· *First*: Take a sheet of paper and write your gut responses to the statement: While I'm still able, I want to _____. Try to jot down fifteen or twenty items. This may take minutes or hours. Allow yourself enough time to plumb your depths.

· *Second*: Go down the list item by item, asking yourself: "Would I be sorry if I never did this one?" If your answer is, "No, I wouldn't be sorry," draw a line through it, because it's not really a priority in your life. It's okay, even necessary, to let go of some of your long-held goals and possibilities.

• ***Third****:* This is a crucial step. Again go down the list of items not crossed off, asking yourself: "If I knew I would die next week, I would most regret not doing _____." Highlight the ones that would cause you regret if left undone. These are your top priorities.

You might categorize what you've done as:

• Highlighted? Essential. Tell yourself, "I'll do this first."

• Neither highlighted nor crossed off? Nice to do, but won't cause regret. "I'll do this if I have time."

• Crossed off? Skip it; not a priority. "I choose to let this one go and not spend time on it."

It should be obvious by now where to focus your time and energy, but how can you get what you want to accomplish off the list and into your everyday life? Choose your top priority, then set the goals which will allow it to come to fruition. Under each goal, write down the specific actions you need to take. Assign a reasonable date by which to accomplish each step, and get busy. Focus on one step at a time so you don't get overwhelmed. You can do this.

You are gifted and the world around you will be diminished if you don't make your unique contribution. Whatever age you are, today's the day to get started, so reach into your spiritual gardening bucket for the seeds of life you've been saving and start planting your future.

35

Be the Catalyst for the Changes You Want in Life

In they came: one recently retired from the military and looking for another way to serve; one at a loss for "next steps" after her thirty-five year marriage ended; another whose husband had committed suicide; yet another who had achieved her dreams and was in search of a new one; plus many who simply yearned to learn more about how to alter the direction of their lives. Altogether, there were twenty women who gathered with me in a circle who needed or wanted to initiate a life change.

To start the discussion, I asked the women to take a quiet moment to "Picture your ideal self. What kind of person would you be? What would you be doing?" A couple women shared their ideal. I shared mine, as well: "I'd be on the New York Times bestseller list, with two more books published since *Second Blooming for Women* came out. I'd have several more articles published, with even more invitations to speak at conferences and women's groups around the country." Then I laughed. "I'm not there yet!"

When I asked if there was a gap between how they saw themselves right now and their ideal self, they all said yes. "Too many women see that gap as imperfection, as a failure, but it isn't," I reassured them. "That gap is where you are able to grow closer and closer to your ideal. You are the best possible person you can be right now, but you will change. The choice is whether you let change just happen *to* you, or you decide you'd rather plan your own path toward your ideal self."

Like all of the women, I don't match my ideal, but I do continue to strive for it. I've spoken to many groups and conferences locally and in a few other states, and will submit my second book to the publisher by the end of this month. Steady progress. I'm satisfied as long as I'm heading in the right direction, remembering that the joy is in the journey.

How can you be the catalyst for the changes you desire in your life? First, believe that you are special, unique, like no woman before or after you. Only you can grow into the woman you were born to be. It doesn't occur by magic, however; you need to be purposeful, have a vision and a plan for yourself. It's very tempting to say, as so many women do, "If only...I had a better job, a more supportive family, more money," and so on, simply wanting the circumstances surrounding them to improve. Wishful thinking. A more productive approach is to tell yourself, "Well, I can wait for my circumstances to change, which they might not, or I can change myself because that's the one thing I can take charge of."

A valuable next step is to learn about yourself in a more detailed, insightful way than you can usually do on your own. Psychology has come a long way in developing useful assessments for us. I'm a fan (and millions of other people are, too) of the VIA Survey of Character Strengths which ranks twenty-four identified strengths.[1] The top five are called your "Signature Strengths." Research has found that the more you focus on using them, the happier and more satisfied you'll be with your life. (Permission hereby granted to stop worrying about your weaknesses!) The survey is free and when you're finished, you can print your results. There are two hundred forty questions which take about thirty minutes to complete. Go to: www.authentichappiness.sas.upenn.edu

Certainly there are many other ways you can learn about yourself, too, but this survey is a great place to start. You may be surprised at your top strengths and excited about finding new ways to use them.

Next, quiz yourself:

• What do I like to do *now*; what gives me pleasure and satisfaction?

• What would I like to be doing in the *future*, say five years from now?

• *Can* I do that; do I have the talents and skills I need? (If you want to sing for crowds but have an ordinary voice, for example, you're unlikely to achieve that goal. Skills can be learned as needed, but biologically based talents can only be polished, not acquired.)

• Am I *willing* to do what it takes to accomplish what I picture for myself?

You've heard the old phrase "Where there's a will, there's a way," but in the growth process, it's better reversed to "a way and a will." Once you picture your ideal self, assess the *way* (options, path) you have for getting there. Then ask yourself, "Do I have the *will*, the commitment, dedication and fortitude to do this?" Most women can easily picture what they want; some of them figure out the way; but few actually have the will to do the essential work. Decide to be one of the few.

The perfect time to be the catalyst for the changes you want in life is *now*, so start growing purposefully toward that beautiful picture you have of your ideal self.

1. Martin E. P. Seligman, Ph.D., *Authentic Happiness* (New York: Free Press, 2002), 134-160.

ABOUT THE AUTHOR

*K*athleen's life has encompassed many twists and turns, each requiring her to adapt by expanding her knowledge and skills. She has been an elementary school teacher, naval officer, writer and speaker on military deployments, counselor, college instructor, coordinator of a hospital-based employee assistance program, and published author and speaker. She conducts seminars for businesses, civic organizations, and nonprofit groups on such topics as stress management, team building, and dealing with changes and transitions. Marriage to a career military officer ensured she was an "expert" on change as they have lived in Monterey, California (where they met); Virginia Beach, Virginia; San Diego, California; Yokosuka, Japan; Washington, D.C.; and finally Pensacola, Florida.

Since the 2010 publication of *Second Blooming for Women: Growing a Life that Matters after Fifty* written with her friend Betsy Smith, Kathleen frequently meets with groups of women to discuss such important life topics as body image, everyday courage, growing older, and trust. These discussions have had a positive impact on her as well as the other women.

Kathleen's article on "The Emotional Cycle of Deployment" was published in Naval Institute *Proceedings* in 1987. Reprints of it continue to be used throughout the United States military services, in Canada and Britain, and it has been translated into several foreign languages. Her articles have been published in magazines, including: *Toastmaster, On the Coast,* and Council on Aging of West Florida's *Coming of Age.* She also writes a column for The Transition Network, a national organization for women over fifty, for their monthly online newsletter.

A bachelor's degree in education, a master's degree

in management, and a master's in marriage and family therapy form the solid academic underpinnings for Kathleen's work. The undergraduate classes she taught included: Introduction to Psychology, Principles and Practices of Counseling, Marriage and Family (her favorite), and Social Psychology. Everyday life, however, has been her most important teacher. She has found life after fifty to be the most exciting and gratifying stage so far, and wants women of all ages to share that same sense of anticipation, adventure and satisfaction along the way.

Kathleen is married to C. Flack Logan; they have one son who is married and has two daughters.

ACKNOWLEDGMENTS

$\mathscr{I}$ am grateful to my family, friends, colleagues, and hundreds of women whose lives have touched mine, whether individually, in workshops, or online. Thank you to my writers' group, *Write On! Pensacola*, whose members have listened to most of these pieces over the years, giving me invaluable feedback for improving them.

Rob Engel has generously shared his computer expertise, helping me navigate the sometimes bewildering world of Windows 8.1 on a new computer. He also managed the move of the *Second Blooming for Women* website to a new provider with greater security. I appreciate his prompt replies to calls for help, his many skills, steady guidance, and especially his infinite patience.

Nancy Cleary expressed enthusiasm for this book which is quite different from the first one published with my co-author Betsy Smith, *Second Blooming for Women: Growing a Life that Matters after Fifty*, in 2010. Nancy is knowledgeable, encouraging, responsive, and once again has used her graphic skills to create a lovely book.

Debbie Tracy, owner of Angel's Garden Gift Shop in Pensacola, Florida, has become a wonderful friend since we first met in 2010 and started hosting guided conversations for women at her store. She has helped bring together many women in our community who attend the sessions, sharing their experiences and wisdom. Their insightful comments enrich the content of this book.

I extend a special thank you to The Transition Network (TTN) for inviting me to contribute columns to their monthly online newsletter since 2010. I would submit them first to Carole Holland, who frequently had thoughtful responses to the material because our lives intersected sometimes in unexpected ways. Betsy Werley served as Executive Director for several years, followed by Susan Collins. This book would not exist without the support of the TTN staff and the members.

Finally, I'm especially grateful to my beloved husband, Flack. He was my biggest supporter, cheering me on when my motivation flagged or I became frustrated. He honors the work I do, often telling me I'm having a positive impact on people's lives. That is my wish and my purpose, but he helps make it happen.

IN CLOSING

My nephew's daughter, Allison Vestal, is ten and loves to draw. When she heard about this book, she wanted to draw a picture for it. She captures the spirit of *Women's Wisdom* perfectly. If we just hold hands and love each other, we can *Pass It On!*

CPSIA information can be obtained at www.ICGtesting.com
Printed in the USA
LVOW02s1304190515

439023LV00003B/3/P